ROUTLEDGE LIBRARY EDITIONS: THE AMERICAN NOVEL

Volume 2

THE ASSIMILATION EXPERIENCE OF FIVE AMERICAN WHITE ETHNIC NOVELISTS OF THE TWENTIETH CENTURY

THE ASSIMILATION EXPERIENCE OF FIVE AMERICAN WHITE ETHNIC NOVELISTS OF THE TWENTIETH CENTURY

BETTY ANN BURCH

Routledge
Taylor & Francis Group
LONDON AND NEW YORK

First published in 1990 by Garland Publishing, Inc.

This edition first published in 2018
by Routledge
2 Park Square, Milton Park, Abingdon, Oxon OX14 4RN

and by Routledge
711 Third Avenue, New York, NY 10017

Routledge is an imprint of the Taylor & Francis Group, an informa business

British Library Cataloguing in Publication Data
A catalogue record for this book is available from the British Library

ISBN: 978-1-138-09946-3 (Set)
ISBN: 978-1-351-25544-8 (Set) (ebk)
ISBN: 978-1-138-50181-2 (Volume 2) (hbk)
ISBN: 978-1-138-50184-3 (Volume 2) (pbk)
ISBN: 978-1-315-14457-3 (Volume 2) (ebk)

The Assimilation Experience of Five American White Ethnic Novelists of the Twentieth Century

Betty Ann Burch

Garland Publishing, Inc. • New York & London • 1990

Library of Congress Cataloging-in-Publication Data

Burch, Betty Ann.
The assimilation experience of five American white ethnic novelists of the twentieth century/ Betty Ann Burch.
p. cm.—(European immigrants and American society)
Includes bibliographical references.
ISBN 0-8240-7423-8 (alk. paper)
1. Authors, American—20th century—Biography.
2. American fiction—Minority authors—History and criticism. 3. Ethnicity in literature. 4. American fiction—20th century—History and criticism. I. Title. II. Series.
PS153.M56B87 1990
813'.509—dc20 90-39828
[B]

Printed on acid-free, 250-year-life paper.
Manufactured in the United States of America

Design by
Julie Threlkeld

Preface

The publication of Dr. Betty Ann Burch's dissertation seventeen years after it was written is long overdue, but nonetheless welcome. It was conceived as a contribution to a redefinition of American literature, one which would be inclusive of the many voices that have made up the polyphony (and sometimes cacophony) of these United States of America. As such it was a pioneering work in the still ongoing debate over the criteria by which to decide what writings should be included in the canon. What, after all, is American literature? and who is an American writer? And most importantly, by what standards, aesthetic, stylistic, social, ideological, are works to be judged as worthy of being read, taught, indeed, published?

The past two decades have seen a widespread, although hardly universal, acceptance of a pluralistic perspective on American history and culture. Anglo-conformity has been rejected as a descriptive—and even moreso as a normative—model for determining what is American; and the Melting Pot, although refurbished during the Reagan reign, has quite a few dents in it. But this was hardly true when Betty Ann Burch began work on her dissertation. A challenge to the Americanization motif had been raised by the events of the sixties: the Black Power movement; the anti-Vietnam war movement; the student movement; the feminist and sexual liberation movements. Together these movements constituted a revolution with cultural as well as political ramifications. If it appears that in some respects this was a failed revolution (after all, it ushered in the administrations of Nixon, Reagan, and Bush), in other respects (values, lifestyles) it transformed America. However, in the early seventies, when Dr. Burch was in the throes of doctoral studies, these outcomes were still undecided. This study is thus itself significant as a cultural document of the times. With her dissertation, Dr. Burch entered forcefully into the controversy over the significance of ethnicity in shaping American history—and literature.

The Black pride and consciousness movement of the sixties was in the forefront in the assault on the academic strongholds of the Anglo-American establishment. Black Studies programs sprang up on university campuses around the country. A revaluation of the African American experience inevitably resulted in a rediscovery of the writings of African Americans, and the demand that they be included in American literature courses and anthologies. The examples of successful Black incursions into the Anglo-American literary monopoly inspired other excluded segments of society to emulate them. Women as well as other "racial" groups—Chicanos, American Indians, and Asian Americans—not only discovered their voices in writings by forebears, but demanded that this literature be validated and dignified by inclusions in the canon. The resulting controversy continues to reverberate in the precincts of the National Endowment for the Humanities, foundations, and universities.

What perhaps came as a surprise to many (certainly historians and social scientists) was the alacrity and militancy with which "white ethnic" groups also proclaimed their collective identities ("Polish [or Irish, or Swedish, etc.] is Beautiful") and sought to manifest their particular histories and cultures. These "white ethnics" (a term that I too was guilty of using at the time, but now think is a misnomer) were the second, third, or more generation descendants of European immigrants, who according to the melting pot ideology ought to have been totally assimilated by now. Instead, here they were demanding that their voices also be heard through the novels, poetry, and art they had created as part of the chorus of America. This study, which deals with five American "white ethnic" novelists, can be thought of as a response to that demand. As Dr. Burch observed, "the stirrings of the seventies demand that we reread these books. . . ."

Dr. Burch placed her study within the context of the immigrant experience, viewing these writers as all wrestling with the typical second generation conflict of identities. She reads the texts from this perspective, interrogating them with regard to questions of marginality, assimilation, and ethnicity. How, she asks, did these children of immigrants come to terms with the duality between their Old World familial cultures and the New World realities? How, through their literary expressions, did they resolve the dilemma? How did they choose? And how can these texts inform our understanding of the processes of adjustment and acculturation and of the pain and cost as well as the gain and joy involved? Not surprisingly many of these writings also deal with the world of work. Again Dr. Burch examines them to explore the lives of workingclass people and their struggles as members of labor organizations. She is also concerned with the portrayal of women in the novels. Not all the works deal with all of these themes, but a substantial portion do.

Dr. Burch does not claim that all of these writers are firstrate novelists nor that all their works are unknown masterpieces. She candidly judges some of the works as excellent, others good, and some not so good. She has a proper appreciation of *Mount Allegro* by Jerre Mangione, which by now in its sixth edition has rightly earned its designation as a classic. And she was one of the few in the seventies to "discover" Thomas Bell's *Out of this Furnace*, the moving saga of three generations of Slovak American steel workers, which she judged among all the books she read as "most fully portray[ing] the immigrant experience." I first learned about this remarkable novel from Dr. Burch, and, thanks to the fact that it was reprinted in 1976, I and many other teachers have since used it as a text in our courses. Ben Field, about whose writings Dr. Burch is enthusiastic, has not fared as well. None of his novels, not even *Jacob's Son*, is in print (perhaps they too are waiting to be "discovered").

But all of the writings, good, bad, and indifferent, are grist for Dr. Burch's mill, which she uses to illuminate the themes outlined above. Although she applies techniques of literary criticism in her analysis, the works for her have a usefulness beyond their quality as belles-lettres. This literature is a way of entering in an intimate, subjective manner the lives of immigrants and workers, and has an intrinsic value in that respect.

The texts themselves, which she summarizes and analyzes in some detail, serve as the major source for Dr. Burch's explorations of these matters. But, in addition, she presents biographies of the writers, seeking connections between their "real" lives and the worlds they created in their imaginations. Dr. Burch also draws effectively upon the correspondence she conducted with the three living authors and the widows of the two who were deceased. These letters, some of which are quoted at length, contain reflections upon their writings by the novelists themselves. Written, often, years after the fact, one wonders how much is retrospective rationalization, but they are nonetheless revealing.

Dr. Burch also examined contemporary reviews of the novels as they appeared. Her discussion of this criticism indicates the very different perspective that obtained in the 1940s as opposed to the 1970s. The issues of marginality and identity that Dr. Burch finds so central to these writings were largely passed over by reviewers at the time. Her query whether the ethnic character of a novel affected decisions by publishers whether to publish or not elicited inconclusive replies, but the comments regarding variations among ethnic groups in book reading (and buying) are suggestive.

Dr. Burch did not undertake this study in a spirit of dispassionate, disinterested scholarship. As her conclusion reveals, she chose to be an advocate of an inclusive American literature that would be a mirror of an inclusive American society. To be excluded from the literature of the country, to be denied a voice, she maintained, was to be excluded from its history and culture, to be inarticulate and invisible. She called for a "new definition of American literature [which] would form a new canon. . . , one which would include the best stories and songs of all the peoples of America. . . ."

How far have we come in the seventeen years since Dr. Burch wrote those words? In some respects we appear to have made a quantum leap. One need only review the list of courses offered by English, American studies, and history departments around the country, scan the reading lists of courses in American literature or history, examine the table of contents of anthologies of American writings, to see the dramatic change in terms of content since 1970. Not only are the writings more inclusive than they were, but so also are the faculties that teach them. For years now universities in their quest (partly ideological, partly political in motivation) to diversify their teaching staffs have avidly pursued the too-few qualified "minority" persons.

Of late an increasing number of institutions of higher education have established curriculum requirements for "cultural pluralism" or "ethnic studies." Undergraduate students in the College of Liberal Arts at the University of Minnesota, for example, are required to take a certain number of courses to satisfy a "cultural pluralism" requirement. However, a course taught by Dr. Burch utilizing the novels in her study would not meet this requirement. The requirement specifies that only courses which focus primarily on Afro-Americans, Asian Americans, American Indians, or Chicanos are acceptable. Such a requirement, however well intended, contradicts the meaning of pluralism as it developed historically and as we understood it in the seventies. At other institutions one finds the same misguided constriction placed on "ethnic studies" to mean studies of "racial minorities." Such a restricted definition of diversity based on a single characteristic, skin color, ignores the historical and contemporary significance of differences stemming from language, religion, and culture, in short, ethnicity. It denies the recognition and respect that are due to all such differences under a true realm of pluralism and condemns the rest of the American people to being simply *white*.

Dr. Burch's conception of pluralism is more generous and expansive. It does not deny to any group its rightful claim to its own distinctive history and culture. And it would include all those distinctive histories and cultures within an inclusive definition of America. Because it strongly asserts that ideological commitment, for that reason as well, I believe that the publication of this study is timely and welcome.

Rudolph J. Vecoli
Professor of History
Director, Immigration History Research Center
University of Minnesota

CONTENTS

PREFACE

I wrote this dissertation in 1973 as a contribution to the social and literary history of ethnic groups in America. Its sources were the writings--chiefly novels--of five members of Eastern and Southern European ethnic groups. I chose these authors because they depicted the acculturation of their people, the meeting of their own ethnic group and American society.

As the children of immigrant parents, they themselves were on the margin between the two cultures. Their home environments were ethnic rather than American. Even though they learned in school the American language, American holidays, American ideals, and some American ways, they could not abandon their heritage.

From their marginal stance, they expressed in fiction what they had observed and experienced, and they wrote symbolically of their journey to a choice of belonging to one group or the other. Descendents of Eastern and Southern Europeans who had come to America in the late nineteenth and early twentieth century were only beginning in the 1930s and 40s to write of their experiences and to have their works published.

Studying the lives and literary works of a handful of novelists could not give definitive answers to the questions of marginality, identity or ethnicity, but such a study was a means of expanding the cultural history of ethnicity in America and served to show also how these questions were pertinent to and a part of American literature.

Brief excerpts from this work pertaining to women in ethnic literature were included in a paper given at a conference on ethnic studies sponsored by Mankato State University in May 1975.

Other portions of this work were included in a paper "East European Writers in America: Four Cases" which I gave at a conference on the East European experience in America at the University of Wisconsin-Milwaukee in May 1979. The paper appears in the proceedings of the conference published in 1980 in the East European Monographs series distributed by Columbia University Press. The four cases were Thomas Bell, Ben Field, Vera Lebedeff, and Richard Bankowsky, a Polish-American novelist of a later generation.

In presenting this study 17 years after its completion, I now know firsthand what Ben Field meant by "digging and scratching in the compost heap" of scholarship done in what seems more than one lifetime ago and truly is two or three careers ago.

I will present some new material here on the subsequent life and works of Vera Lebedeff, Ben Field, and Jerre Mangione and mention the widows of Michael DeCapite and Thomas Bell who graciously assisted me with my work the first time around.

Natalie Whiting DeCapite retired from the Hastings-on-Hudson public school system, remarried, and is now living in Westerly, Rhode Island.

Marie Benedetti Bell gave Thomas Bell's manuscripts, journals, a large number of negatives and prints of photographs that Bell had taken, and a number of books from Bell's collection to Professor David P. Demarest, Jr. in 1980. These materials are now in the Carnegie-Mellon University Library. Marie Bell died in California in early 1987.

Vera Lebedeff, now a widow, is living in Clearwater, Florida. Her book on the Scotch Settlement school in Dearborn, Michigan is yet to be completed.

Ben Field was a teacher and Dean of the Brooklyn Academy, a small private school for boys, before he retired in his late sixties. He died in California in June 1986 leaving a large number of manuscripts in the care of his son, Joseph Bragin.

A memorial to Field "as a writer of distinction," was written by the editor of _Jewish Currents_, Morris U. Schappes. He noted that Field had worked at all the trades he wrote about and quoted from a review praising his authenticity and rich, strong language.

Jerre Mangione is living in Philadelphia and currently at work on a history of the Italians in America. He retired from the University of Pennsylvania in 1977 with the rank of Emeritus Professor.

Since 1973, his writings include two books: _Mussolini's March on Rome_ and _An Ethnic at Large: A Memoir of America in the Thirties and Forties_.

In Chapter 15 of _An Ethnic at Large_, "A Not-So-Final Note," Mangione says he was 35 years old when Franklin Roosevelt died, and "It [his 35th birthday] marked the end of my apprenticeship as an American" (p. 367). It is interesting to note that the protagonist of Mangione's novel _Night Search_ is about 35 years old when he carries out his quest for reality and identity and symbolically turns toward America.

Further on, the "Not-So-Final Note" says, "the children [of immigrants] were left with confused impressions of identity that were never resolved. I resolved mine by becoming an ethnic at large, with one foot in my Sicilian heritage, the other in the American mainstream" (p. 369).

Among the books considered in my study, Mangione's _Mount_

Allegro has been the one with continued fame, being reprinted over and over. Mangione wrote a new chapter "Finale" for the fifth edition in 1981. In 1986, a historical marker was erected in Rochester, New York commemorating the neighborhood of Mount Allegro and Mangione's book about his family and neighbors. The book went into a sixth edition in 1989.

Thomas Bell's _Out of This Furnace_ has been successfully revived. It was reprinted in 1976 by the University of Pittsburgh Press with an Afterword on Bell and his life by Professor Demarest. It has become a best seller among academic press books, having sold 65,000 copies in this edition. It is used in 230 colleges and universities in courses in American history, ethnic history, and labor history.

As Professor Demarest has discovered, it has a number of themes and elements that appeal to many groups--labor historians, union members, and women for example.

An element that appealed to me when I read _Furnace_ in the early 70s was the subtle progression in Bell's description of the Pittsburgh area from a lovely green place to a place of hills and valleys blighted by pollution emanating from the mills and factories. I grew up in an area similarly blighted, so Bell's description had a poignancy for me that may now be felt by others in this more ecology-minded decade of the 90s.

Another element that had appeal for me, because my own mother had been a "hired girl," was Bell's description of Mary Dobrejcak's work as a hired girl in the homes of middle class people and how her contact with that style of life led her to aspire to a better life.

I assigned _Out of This Furnace_ to students in an independent study course on immigration and ethnicity in American life that I taught at Metropolitan State University in St. Paul from 1977 to 1982. Among other study questions, I asked them to inquire if any of their women relatives had worked as hired girls.

Everyone without exception (including a Vietnamese student whose mother had worked in a wealthy home in Saigon) found an older woman in their family with recollections--some pleasant, some bitter--of being a hired girl.

By caring about women and depicting women's work, Thomas Bell opened up a connection between my students and their relatives and also helped them make a connection with women's history that they might not otherwise have made.

As I pointed out in Chapter VI of my study, Thomas Bell anticipated a number of the comments and analyses that Michael Novak wrote in *The Rise of the Unmeltable Ethnics* in 1971. Bell's attention to the deterioration of the natural environment of the Pittsburgh area and his attention to women's lives and the work they did both in their own homes and elsewhere also anticipated interests that were to come along decades after he wrote.

The ending may still be too patriotic for our taste, but the richness of observation, detail, and thought make *Out of This Furnace* stand as a masterpiece of American literature.

As mentioned in Chapter I, The National Council of Teachers of English (NCTE) Task Force on Racism and Bias in the Teaching of English and its 1972 report *Searching for America* helped focus my concern about the rigid canon of American literature. The Task Force is still meeting but has not issued a follow-up or revised its 1972 report.

Some movement has occurred in the canon, but it is difficult to change. Nor is the NCTE able to tell if the Task Force report precipitated whatever change has occurred.

Events of the last decade have reinforced my conclusion that expansion of the canon is needed. The destructive attitude of the federal government and media toward labor unions suggests that the history of labor and novels about the labor movement and the working class need to be read and pondered lest indeed we are condemned to repeat history.

The attention currently focused on the countries and peoples of Eastern Europe recall both Bell's and Michael Novak's discussions of the scant attention given to them in American schools and Novak's comment in a speech given in the Twin Cities that it always seemed mportant for American students to be taught the differences among England, Scotland, and Wales but not the differences among Slovakia, Bohemia, and Moravia.

The revival of Out of This Furnace and its success suggest that it and other books dealing with labor history and the stories of Eastern European peoples in America could help broaden students' understanding of America's plural culture, its history, and their own place in it.

* * * * *

Letters and other materials from the three authors and the two widows and copies of short stories, poems, book reviews, and essays used in the research for this book are housed in the archives of the Immigration History Research Center, University of Minnesota.

ACKNOWLEDGMENTS

This book could not have been completed without the help of scholars and friends and the invaluable cooperation of Marie Benedetti Bell, Natalie Whiting DeCapite, Ben Field, Vera Lebedeff, and Jerre Mangione, who replied with utmost courtesy, enthusiasm, and diligence to my queries in 1972 and 1973. Mangione supplied further facts and clarifications later which led to some revisions of Chapter IV.

Answers to my queries necessitated, as Ben Field wrote, "considerable digging and scratching in the compost heap of faded notebooks, stained manuscripts, and periodicals long out of print . . . strip mining in some places, and in others following a vein like the iron miners of the Mesabi Iron Range, to hell and gone."

I wish to acknowledge recent assistance from Ben Field's son, Joseph Bragin, Associate Dean, School of Natural and Social Sciences, California State University, Los Angeles; Vera Lebedeff's daughter, Judge Diane Alexis Lebedeff, New York Supreme Court, First Judicial District; the staff of the Board of Education, Hastings-on-Hudson, New York for help in locating Natalie DeCapite; and Professor David P. Demarest, Jr., English Department, Carnegie-Mellon University, for information about Marie Bell and the recent history of _Out of This Furnace_.

My continuing gratitude goes to Rudolph J. Vecoli, Professor of History and Director of the Immigration History Research Center, University of Minnesota, who introduced me to ethnic studies and who has since been a mentor, colleague, and friend; to Professor Emerita

Mary C. Turpie, former Director of American studies at the University of Minnesota; to Colleen Coghlan, librarian extraordinaire; to the staff of Wilson Library at the University of Minnesota, who proved once again their enthusiasm for the chase; and to Rita Bienvenue, Canadian sociologist, who gave me a useful perspective on the U.S., its values, politics, and place in the world.

My thanks are extended again to those exemplars of American studies scholarship, Mary Farrell Bednarowski and Gayle Graham Yates; to Roberta K. Gladowski for giving me the benefit of her wide-ranging experiences and thoughts; and to Louise Osojnicki Hiniker, granddaughter of Eastern European immigrants, whose discussions of ethnicity and marginality taught me a great deal about searching for identity.

CHAPTER I

PRINCIPLES AND PURPOSES OF THIS STUDY

Rationale for the study of ethnic literatures in the context of "classic American" literature

As scholars move into ethnic studies, it becomes obvious that the histories and cultures of all ethnic groups in the United States must be explored, so that in time all such groups will be given their rightful place in what has been heretofore a rather restricted cultural mainstream.

As Rudolph J. Vecoli pointed out in his historiographical essay on the ethnic dimension in American history, the necessity exists for a pluralistic view of the American past; the congeries of groups that make up America must be included in the study of our history, and the meaning of the present ethnic composition of our society must be determined.

In discussing the role of academics in ethnic historical studies, Vecoli wrote that "the cultivation of ethnic history might serve as one of the much-needed bridges between the university ghetto and the ethnic ghetto."[1]

In an analogous way, American literature must become more pluralistic. The term "American literature" will have to be redefined to include the literature of many peoples heretofore walled off. White ethnic and racial groups need to be studied from historical, sociological, and anthropological viewpoints, and they can also be viewed from the inside: the view that literature can provide.

In addition, our society will be enriched by knowing the work of writers of many ethnic and racial backgrounds, which portray their values, different solutions to social problems, and many ways of living.

In 1972, the National Council of Teachers of English Task Force on Racism and Bias in the Teaching of English noted the problem: they reported that American literature anthologies "revealed . . . ethnic racism, . . . the emphasis on the Atlantic frontier, the Puritan spirit, and the Cavalier tradition."[2]

They found a small canon of literature, reporting that "current American literature anthologies . . . [reveal] . . . the pattern of reprinting what has been printed before and shunning the otherwise meritorious writer because he has not been previously anthologized."[3]

The Task Force also noted, "American literature anthologies today give students only a skewed and deceptive portrait of American life and letters." They suggested that if teachers, administrators, and publishers act to change these anthologies into "texts that accurately portray the multi-ethnic literary and cultural history of this country" students would "at the very least" be allowed to deal with "the raw materials of truth."[4]

The intention of my study was to find meritorious writers who accurately portrayed the history of their own ethnic people.

Principles of selection of the authors to be studied

The literature of racial and ethnic groups falls broadly into two categories: those works which deal almost exclusively with the group members as they interact among themselves and those which deal with the interactions of group members with members of the society outside their group. These categories are not clear cut, especially in novels in which there is necessarily some contact with the larger society in the persons of employers, salespersons, or neighbors. An example of both kinds of interaction is Henry Roth's Call It Sleep. Events in this novel are largely contained within the Jewish family group, but the action leading to the climax of the book is precipitated by the neighbor boy, Leo, who is a Catholic.

Examples of novels which deal mainly with one group are O. E. Rolvaag's Giants in the Earth, James T. Farrell's Studs Lonigan, Pietro DiDonato's Christ in Concrete, and more recently Raymond Barrio's The Plum Plum Pickers. A small list of short stories in this first category would be: Prudencio de Pereda's "The Conquistador," Ralph Ellison's "Did You Ever Dream Lucky?" Bienvenido Santos' "The Day the Dancers Came," Ferris Takahashi's "The Widower," Durango Mendoza's "Summer Water and Shirley," a story about Indians, and the whole series of stories about Jesse Semple by Langston Hughes.

Examples of works in the second category, those in which members of an ethnic group interact with the larger society, are Ralph Ellison's Invisible Man, Ossie Davis' play Purlie Victorious, Piri Thomas' Down These Mean Streets, short stories such as Emerson Blackhorse Mitchell's "Miracle Hill," and Emilio Diaz Vilcarcel's "Damian Sanchez, G.I."

Works of the first kind aid readers in understanding the mores and Weltanschauung of a racial or ethnic group. The works in the second category may give some of that same understanding, but they also give insight into group contact and group conflict, into the place of a given ethnic group in American society.

Ethnic authors have written more than the story of their own people, however; in addition, they have depicted how their group viewed the American society they confronted and how they reacted to it. These authors wrote out of their own experience, depicting their ethnic milieu, and also depicting the larger society as they perceived it. Through the characters they invented, they show their own lives--and symbolically, the possibilities for meeting and coming to terms with America. Those who were the children of the immigrant generation, especially, had to come to terms with their own identity in American society. They were the marginal generation coping with their ambivalent status.

Some of these writers wrote of their own people with warmth and love, seeing them move slowly into American society and beginning to reap its economic benefits. And--more important--they saw their people helping to bring to reality the American ideals they had been taught in school and had learned from their parents' yearnings.

Other writers held their own people in esteem and saw the American Dream as acceptance of middle-class achievement, a dream to be fulfilled by leaving the ethnic group behind. Still others wrote as one suspended between America and Europe until finally choosing America, but with persistent memories of their childhood's painful dilemma.

At the beginning of my work in ethnic history in 1969, my own background as a native of a city whose population is heavily Eastern and Southern European prompted me to concentrate on the history of immigrants from Eastern and Southern Europe and, later, to begin the study of novels about them, especially those written by their children. These immigrants were part of the last great wave of immigration; they were the so-called "New Immigrants" of the latter part of the nineteenth century and the early decades of the twentieth.

The authors chosen were children of immigrants and were born at about the same time, between 1900 and 1910. They produced much of their work at about the same time, principally during the decade of the forties. They or their parents belonged to the working class and were on the lowest rung of the American mobility ladder. They wrote from a proletarian point of view, deliberating upon and delineating the problems of the working class in their writings, fiction and non-fiction.

After wide reading of novels by members of these New Immigrant groups, my field of study was narrowed to five authors. Some ethnic authors of both Old and New Immigration wrote about identity and--as discussed above--of their own group interacting internally and with the society at large. Not all ethnic writers did so, nor did all of them deal with all of those themes. These five writers were chosen because they did deal with those themes and because their work has the literary quality to make the study and possible revival of it worthwhile from the literary standpoint as well as from sociological and historical views. Even among the five, however, the literary quality varies, as will be noted when each author's work is discussed.

The five include Michael DeCapite and Jerre Mangione, who are of Italian origin; Thomas Bell (né Belejcak) who was of Slovak origin; Vera Lebedeff, a Russian; and Ben Field (né Moses Bragin) a Russian Jew. Some of these writers were more prolific than others, but the less prolific deal with the problems of ethnicity and assimilation so well that they deserve inclusion on the basis of only one or two novels.

In an article on ethnic writers, Myron Simon gave "some necessary qualifications" in his attempted definition of "ethnic writer." One of these qualifications is that

> it is necessary to distinguish between ethnic writers who serve a largely documentary function and those who use ethnic materials metaphorically, to embody fictions whose meanings transcend their materials. What a growing number of ethnic writers now know is that they must, as writers, extend their vision to its furthest limits, to a perception of the contingency that frames all human action, making easy judgments impossible.[5]

Simon is apparently thinking only of writers currently at work. The writers I am considering wrote in the 1940's, for the most part, but they, too, had a vision that embodied more than the history or mores of their own group. They wrote of the proletarian movements of the thirties and forties, the problems of the working poor in America, and of even more universal themes: family relationships, human growth and maturation, and the development of integrity, responsibility, and compassion.

But rather than using their ethnic materials metaphorically, as Simon suggests contemporary writers must do, they often submerged the ethnic dimension (using Anglo-Saxon names for their characters was one way) still dealing, however, with the problems of family life, adolescent rebellion and maturation, and the responsibility of the individual to make his society more responsive to ideals of freedom and justice.

As Mumford Jones noted in 1941, the writers among

> the newer American stocks . . . have concerned themselves with the ways by which the newer races have been, or are being, assimilated into the life of the United States. . . . They do not complain, these authors, except when the promise of American life has not been fulfilled.[6]

In a later analysis of the fiction of the forties, Chester Eisinger stated that "the quest for the self was intensified in the fiction of this decade . . . in such a way as to assume the proportions of a movement."[7] The five authors in this study were concerned with that quest, also, possibly more so than others, because of their marginal status as the children of immigrants. All of them wrote about American identity or identity as such in the forties and beyond. Each of them also wrote at least one novel about the acculturation or assimilation of their people. They demonstrated that they thought deeply about their own identity as members of despised or little known ethnic groups, as Americans, and as human beings. From their marginal viewpoint as second generation Americans, they depicted American society and what it means to be an autonomous person in that society; i.e., to make an identity for one's self and yet not become isolated from family or community.

These five men and women were faced with the task of choosing an identity among the possibilities open to the child of immigrant parents: a return to the homeland (real or symbolic), a commitment to America, or a state of indecision in which the person is not assimilated or committed to America and yet has lost a sense of real attachment to the homeland of his parents. Vera Lebedeff concentrated on describing these three possibilities. Her method is to flesh them out as characters in her novel _The Heart Returneth_. In order to allow her analysis to provide a frame of reference for the following discussions, the chapter on Lebedeff is placed first in the body of this dissertation.

In order to utilize works of fiction as documents for historical study, it was necessary to study the lives of the writers as well as their work. Through such a study, it became obvious that each author had to face the question of marginality. Each faced it, and each expressed in his or her work that dilemma and its solution, his or her choice of identity. The following chapters will detail the life and work of each of the five novelists and the conclusion I reached as to their choice of identity. Briefly stated, Vera Lebedeff, Michael DeCapite, and Thomas Bell chose to be committed to America; Jerre Mangione and Ben Field moved rather late in life from uncommitted to committed.

These conclusions are based on biographical data and on a critical analysis of the body of works written by these five persons. Most of the work of reading, criticism, and analysis was completed before I consulted the three authors still living and the widows of the other two. I sent each of them a series of questions based on the tentative conclusions I had already reached. The function of the questions was to provide biographical data and other information which could not be learned from printed sources; corroboration of insights gained from my analysis, and opinions about the climate of acceptance when their writings were first put on the market. The respondents volunteered additional bibliography which had not appeared in any of the standard reference sources or short lists of works included in biographical blurbs in magazines or collections of stories. All of the respondents, except Lebedeff, answered my questions fully and frankly. These completed questionnaires are referred to in citations as "personal letters," with a date where necessary to distinguish one group of answers from another. (In order to speed the process of getting their answers to me, some of the respondents sent a few answers one day and the rest another. Cover letters often contained pertinent material, also.)

Analytical tools

Many of the literary critic's tools were utilized, including analysis of point of view and the symbolic interpretation of names, places, and events. An example of the symbolism of names is found in Mangione's novel Night Search: the narrator, searching for the murderer of his Sicilian father, journeys to Cape Cod, where he meets and falls in love with a girl named Lucy Hawthorne. "Hawthorne" is surely a name that can be associated with old stock America; thus, this bit of evidence, along with others, suggests the beginning of commitment to America.

"Point of view" has been defined as "the vantage point from which the author presents the actions of the story." It is considered by many critics since Henry James as "the technical aspect of fiction which leads the critic most readily into the problems and the meanings of a novel or short story."[8] Whether an author chooses a first person narrator or a third person central intelligence, for example, he is creating what has been called a persona, mask, or second self through whom he tells his story. The critical importance of the persona is implicit in this comment, "All fiction is in some sense a story told by someone; all self-consciously artistic fiction is told by someone created by the author and who serves, therefore, as a mask, a persona."[9]

After the critical analysis of each piece of work, an interpretation of each author's body of work was undertaken. It was, figuratively, to stand back and view the works as a whole, as one story rather than separate stories. The biography of each novelist was utilized to relate his or her life to what he wrote about his characters and about America: first, to observe how much of his own life was incorporated into his works, and, second, to speculate on his or her own relationship to America and what identity he or she chose.[10]

Purpose of the study

The works of these authors appeared mainly in the forties, but they need to be reread now that many groups in American society are revaluating their heritage, their experience, their present status in American society, and the contributions their people have made to this country. These books were reviewed as they were published, but the reviewers were not attuned to them as we are in trying to understand ethnicity and the full place in American history of all of the ethnic groups. The stirrings of the seventies demand that we reread these books; the point of view of the ethnic historian will help us focus on the qualities in them that can fulfill the needs of this and subsequent decades for the full story of the American people.

The question of using works of fiction as historical documents can be answered by noting that the skills of the literary critic can aid us in finding the psychological dimension of history. Eisinger quotes Flaubert that "novels are the mirror of their age."

He expands upon this comment:

> [novels] reflect for us the inner face of their time and the impulses and conflicts, both conscious and unconscious, that contain its history. . . . But fiction will lead us beyond a knowledge of the time; it will lead us also to a sense of the self afoot at that time.[11]

Theodore Blegen, the historian, also felt that works of fiction can be historically accurate, saying that the "novelist has often done better than the historian."[12] He had been more explicit in an earlier work:

> We must turn to fiction, however, rather than to history for an adequate treatment of the interrelationship between [the two creative forces of the European heritage and the American environment]; and it is worth noting that the power of such a novel as Giants in the Earth lies not so much in its portrayal of the external scene as in its understanding of the psychological realities underlying the struggle of the immigrants.[13]

Identity is as much a matter of concern now as it was in the forties, perhaps even more so: identity as an American in the global village; identity as a group member who is reaching for autonomous personhood; and identity as a prelude to commitment, as Margaret Mead elucidated in 1970.[14] To read books by these white ethnic authors of an earlier generation is to learn how that generation analyzed and tried to solve the identity problem.

The identity of women as persons is a major focus now, and some of these authors were ahead of their time in depicting women as persons as important as men in searching for personal growth and American ideals, if not as actively engaged in promoting those ideals.

The emergence of racial studies--black, Chicano, American Indian--is beginning to pique other groups to study and disseminate the heritage and the literature of their people. Michael Novak was moved to ask, "What books by Czechs, Slovaks, Poles, and Roumanians have been translated by American scholars and brought into curricula for students of Slavic background?"[15] The American Jewish Historical Society, to cite another example, recently called upon the National American Studies Faculty to aid them in preparing plans for a Jewish Studies curriculum for high schools. They were responding to inquiries as well as following their own wish to disseminate historical materials about their people.

The peoples of southern and eastern European origin are still, in the main, members of the working class. As many young people from that class enter the declassing milieu of higher education, they, too, will want to learn of the earlier life of their forebears in the contexts of American history and literature. In the 1940's Thomas Bell criticized the lack of reality in his public school education, which contained nothing about the Slovak workers in the steel towns.

The following chapters will describe not only what five authors wrote about the "external scene" but will attempt also to further the "understanding of the psychological realities underlying the struggle of the immigrants" and their children for self-realization.

CHAPTER II

VERA LEBEDEFF--MARGINALITY, THE CHOICES OF IDENTITY

Biography

Vera Lebedeff, whose novel The Heart Returneth is almost a paradigm of the theories about the assimilation experience, was herself an immigrant. She had always wanted to be a writer, but she had to spend many years in study and preparation before she could write a story of her own experience and with the insights of sociology.

Lebedeff was born in Kozatin, near Kiev, Russia. During her childhood, she witnessed the beheading of a beloved relative; the emotional shock resulted in a fifty per cent hearing loss, from which she has never recovered. When she was about eight years old, she was brought to the United States by Anthony and Olga Sahulko along with their own two children. They used the birth certificate of their dead child to smuggle Vera into this country, because of severe immigration restrictions. Such deceptions were widespread in those days of war, revolution, and famine. The Sahulkos belonged to wealthy and distinguished Czech families which had fled to the Ukraine during the rebellion of 1848 in Austria-Hungary.[1]

At first she attended public school in Detroit, but later she was transferred to the Scotch Settlement school in Dearborn, Michigan. In that "turbulent and nostalgic first year," she writes, "a lot of us little 'Pollacks' (which word lumped all foreigners) began our Americanization in a garagetown at the edge of the rural and inbred Scotch Settlement."[2] Later she attended Northwestern High school in Detroit and studied at Marygrove College for two years.

In 1932 she married Alexis Lebedeff, a lawyer. She subsequently began taking courses in the social sciences at Wayne State University with a goal of undertaking graduate work in sociology, because, as she said later, "a thorough study of social sciences seemed to me the only means of arriving at some adequate concept of life."[3] It is not surprising that she was seeking concepts of society and an explanation for human behavior. Her early life was spent in the almost feudal culture of the Russian landowner. Her stepmother and stepfather's orientation, however, was to Czech culture. They read Czech newspapers from Chicago and classics of world literature translated into Czech. In addition, Olga Sahulko spent many hours telling what are known as "stories told at the mother's knee," which were actual incidents from Czech history.

Lebedeff herself explains the possible effects of such upbringing.

> And I have wondered since, this type of indoctrination by foreign-born mothers passed onto their American-born children (as it was for about the first two generations here), did it not direct the imaginations, and even the identities of these children, elsewhere--to causes, histories, heroes, that were no longer valid for them? The hyphenated American of my youth was a kind of cultural schizophrenic, very much aware that he was an unwelcome outsider here (as he was) and yet, however much he felt himself a Pole (or Czech or whatever) he was not really that either.[4]

During her years at Wayne, she also studied art, dramatics, and ballet. Her novel The Heart Returneth, published in April, 1943, was based on her own experiences, those of her stepfather, then a tool and die maker in the Ford plant, and of many other White Russians in Detroit. At this time, Lebedeff had planned and partially written another book about the Americanization process at the Scotch Settlement. She dropped out of Wayne State that year because she was expecting a baby.

The Heart Returneth began as an assignment for a cultural anthropology course at Wayne and then grew into the novel. The theme, according to Lebedeff, is

> the adjustment of the White Russians to an alien culture. I wanted to get the feeling of the exile away from home, in a country where the culture is foreign to you and in a way always will be foreign. The story begins in 1941 and is the adjustment of the Russian colony to this new war.[5]

By 1965 Lebedeff had progressed in the art of portrait sculpture through study at the Detroit Society of Arts and Crafts so that a number of her portrait busts were included in a Christmas art sale sponsored by the Dearborn Arts and Crafts Club. By this time she had graduated from Wayne at the top of her class with a major in pyschology and sociology.

The problem of Americanization has been a lifelong concern of Vera Lebedeff. Many people have written about that experience, but a special value of her work is that this novel was written from a sociological viewpoint. Her examination of her own experiences and the experiences of her compatriots was sharpened by her study of sociology,[6] and the resulting narrative is a structuring of the behaviors she observed. Her individual characters are embodiments of the behavior of certain groups. It is this paradigmatic fictionalization which makes her novel not only a literary work but a sociological study. Her novel gives her readers typical behavior, not merely the behavior of the characters as individuals.

The major correspondence between Lebedeff's life and the lives of the characters in her novel is, of course, that she was writing of her own people, but there are other correspondences, too. One of her main characters, Andre, is a lawyer, as is her husband. Prince Lucian, another major figure in the novel, works at an automobile plant, as did Lebedeff's stepfather. Princess Xenya is an artist, as is Lebedeff herself. A 1965 interview mentions that she was working on a book about the Scotch Settlement school. In June, 1972, Lebedeff was "polishing up, hopefully for the last time" that same book.[7] She has a son, who is a doctor, and a daughter, who is a lawyer. She has lived in Dearborn until recently but travels quite frequently.

Discussion of work

Vera Lebedeff's novel <u>The Heart Returneth</u> portrays an unusual immigrant group, the upper-class White Russian émigrés in Detroit. The word "émigré" is used throughout the book; the word suggests the educational level and elitist attitude of these people.

Some of the characters in the book still bear their titles of Prince and Baron; some are former wealthy landowners, and all treat each other with the deference due to their respective stations, even though all of them belong to the American working class, earning their living as salesmen or factory workers.

The émigrés had not chosen to leave their homeland as immigrants do; they had been forced to flee because of political and social turmoil. Even though they lived in America all the rest of their lives, they never tried to gain a place in American society comparable to their status at home. They lived in the expectation that the Bolsheviks' rule over Russia would soon end. This hope was reinforced by the anti-Communist attitude in American political circles at that time and by the media.[8] Among the second generation émigrés, those who were brought from Russia as children, there were some who have educated themselves and gone on to become professional people--lawyers, engineers, artists, and, in one case, a dress designer. But even among them, a sense of not belonging in this country and a nostalgia for the old home sapped their psychic energy and removed any motivation they might have had to achieve in this society what they were capable of. The novel tells the story of three of these second generation émigrés working out their identity as Russians in America. Prince Lucian and the twins, Anna and Andre, embody the three choices that each immigrant has: to return to the old country, to accept America wholeheartedly, or to hang suspended, never quite making the choice of allegiance or fulfilling one's promise.

Prince Lucian is the symbol of the first possibility. He has worked in an auto factory while earning an engineering degree in night school. During World War II two Russian engineers come to this factory to learn American methods, and Lucian is assigned to teach them. He discusses politics and current conditions in Russia with these dedicated Communists. He does not change his political views, but he accepts their offer of a position in a Russian tank factory, because he feels duty-bound to return and aid his beloved homeland, endangered by Hitler's attack.

Prince Lucian had always been a sojourner in America. Even though he was among the younger group of émigrés, his high rank and saintly personality symbolized the best in Imperial Russia for all of the émigrés, old and young. As a touchstone for the colony, he had never lost his Russian identity nor his hope for the return of the old ways even under Russia's new leaders.

Anna, on the other hand, makes a successful transition between the old world and the new, using vocational mobility as her avenue to identity as an American. Even though she is the daughter of an upper-bourgeois family, she has struggled and worked her way up from seamstress to dress designer in a fashionable Detroit store. When she is offered a position as dress designer in the New York shop under the same ownership, she accepts, taking her mother and uncle with her when she moves. Lebedeff makes it clear that Anna is no longer subservient to these elders, tied by a sense of duty, or made immobile by nostalgia for Russia. The scenes here are similar to the scene in the film Rachel, Rachel when Rachel invites her mother to move to another town with her; Rachel has become the leader and her mother the follower. The following passage best illustrates Anna's feeling of freedom and release from old allegiances.

> But always she was the young daughter helping to tide the family over an emergency. . . . The unchanging situation at home remained like a knot tied tight about her. But now the knot was broken. And Anna was resolved that it should never be retied. For they could not hold Andre over her head any longer; or weak hearts, or family peace and affections. She was immune to them all. How long she had felt like this she did not know, but it must have been very long, because the indifference was lodged so solidly within her.
>
> But it was not this prospect of release from old restraints that so delighted Anna, as the anticipation of her new work. At last she was to have the dignity, the self-expression, that she craved. Anna felt herself on the threshold of the life she had always desired, in the America of today. Not for her the yesterdays that haunted the Russian colony of Detroit, and must haunt every émigré community and every exiled soul in the world. Not for her the yesterdays any more.[9]

Anna and the others are barely settled in New York when they receive word that Andre is ill. His wife Louise, who had been attending school in New York, appeals to Anna for advice as to whether or not to reveal that she and Andre are secretly married. Anna solves Louise's dilemma by advising her to go to Detroit and Andre. Anna thus makes concrete her freedom from family ties, her self-awareness, and her identity as an American. Lebedeff indicates this new awareness and identity in another glimpse into Anna's feelings.

> Today she had discharged her last obligation toward Andre.
>
> She was walking back to the shop alone. At last everything in the family was changed. It would never, never be the same again. Through her decision, and on her own responsibility, she had done for Andre what Andre had lacked the courage to do for himself. [Reveal his marriage to Louise.] She was strong. She had never known what power was until now. She had the strength to direct her own life, and the lives of others. . . .
>
> She was aware of the crowds that surged along the street, and the heavy New York traffic, and the buildings that towered above her. She was swept by an exultant sensation. This was her own world and her home. She belonged to it. She was part of its vigor and greatness. She had fought for and won her true place in this world.[10]

Andre, who embodies the third possibility that Lebedeff sees for the immigrant, lives in America suspended between old world and new. Andre is Anna's twin; he has become a lawyer with her help. He has not had courage enough to tell his family that he is married to Louise, an American-born Russian girl. One of the reasons he does not acknowledge this marriage is that his love for Louise is fading. When he meets the Princess Xenya, who symbolizes the pride of old Russia to Andre and the rest of the émigré colony, he has a passionate affair with her.

Near the end of the novel, Andre makes an attempt to end this affair and free himself from Xenya and the clinging memories of his childhood in Russia. When his family had moved to New York, he had chosen to remain in Detroit to follow his profession. For a short time after they leave, he feels free, no longer bound by the limitations placed on him by his mother and uncle. Andre becomes ill; his wife returns to Detroit, reveals their marriage, and takes Andre to her father's home.

Andre recovers from the critical stage of his illness, but he does not regain his feeling of freedom. He cannot embrace Louise but neither does he have the psychic energy to pursue Xenya. He remains in a listless, half-convalescent state, which symbolizes his permanent fixation of spirit. He cannot choose either Louise or Xenya, who symbolize his new life and his old one, his new country and his homeland.

Though Xenya is not one of the major characters, her presence adds richness to the book because she acts as a foil to both Anna and Andre, underlining and pointing up their personalities and actions. Xenya enters the émigré colony during the course of the story. She never makes it clear to the other émigrés where she had been between the time of the Revolution and her arrival among them. She is a powerful symbol to them because of this mystery surrounding her, because of her beauty, and because her father had had a powerful but ambiguous position in Imperial Russia.

The emotion of the Detroit émigrés almost forces Xenya to cling to her Russianness. She is inclined to join Lucian when he decides to return to Russia, but she chooses to remain in Detroit as a symbol for her friends. She chooses to be a Russian in America; she is thus neither Russian nor American. She is suspended by choice; Andre is suspended by lack of choice.

Xenya is an artist, who makes her living with her art, as does Anna, but Xenya's most deeply felt work is an evocation of old Russia. Anna's art is more practical; her designs are contrived purposefully to suit each client. She incorporates hints of Russian folk art in these dresses and makes a name for herself for her cleverness and originality. Her art is client-centered and elegant, and yet it contains elements of her own former life. She utilizes her skill and talent and her past to create new designs for her clients and a new life for herself. Xenya cannot forget her past even in her paintings. Anna does not entirely forget it, either, but she incorporates the past into the present, in her dress designing as in her life. She is an American at the end of the story, but she still has her past with her in the persons of her mother and uncle and in the elements of Russian design.

The Heart Returneth is well written and detailed enough to give a good group-portrait of a hot-house enclave of unsettled persons. It also portrays in fictional form not only the sociological but the psychological and emotional choices that can be made by an immigrant.

Conclusion

In answer to my queries, Lebedeff supplied some biographical data and rather full comments on the psychological state of nostalgia and "marking time" among the émigrés she knew:

> the younger generation (ourselves, alas!) were trying to live a here-&-now [sic] life--none of us too

> successfully--whereas our parents spent the rest of their lives "way back when." They just never managed to relate to post-revolutionary life in America. And the rest of us did so only partially.[11]

She did not answer all of my queries, so I am not able to discuss her own state of mind about herself as a marginal person. My surmise is that she is portrayed--to a certain extent--in Anna Borodin, perhaps only as a wish fulfillment. Further, it is possible that this novel was a cathartic laying out of the problem of marginality rather than a solution. It also may be true that her unsuccessful attempt to live in the here and now was a life lacking the serenity necessary for sustained creative work.

CHAPTER III

MICHAEL DECAPITE--THE TRANSCENDENCE OF AMERICAN IDENTITY

Biography

Michael DeCapite spent most of his life as a writer, reporting for newspapers, disseminating information for the United Nations, and expressing in fiction his own story and his ideas and feelings about America. He was born on April 13, 1915 in Cleveland, Ohio, the son of an Italian-born father and a second generation Italian mother.

His father was from the village of Rivisondoli in the Abruzzi and came to America when he was fourteen. He worked on railroad gangs. He had little schooling, but he believed in education for his children, at one time purchasing for them a large, unabridged dictionary. DeCapite's mother was born Carrie LaGratta in Cleveland. She worked on an NRA sewing project during the Depression and for many years as a checker at Sears. She and DeCapite's brother and sister still live in Cleveland.[1]

DeCapite graduated from Lincoln High School in Cleveland in 1933 and then tried to find employment. Failing that, he entered Ohio University in Athens, where he majored in English and became acquainted with many campus radicals. He graduated--a member of Phi Beta Kappa--in 1938. The same year, he had a short story "Honesty" published in the Lamplighter magazine.

He and his wife Natalie, whom he had met at Ohio University, were married in an Episcopal church on March 25, 1939. DeCapite had been raised a Catholic, but left the church after becoming disenchanted with what he saw as political and hypocritical in it. He worked for a few months in 1939 on the City Desk at the City News Bureau in Chicago. In the fall, he went to New York University on a fellowship and did graduate work in the history of architecture and philosophy in the Fine Arts Department. His interest in Louis Sullivan, as architect of a democracy, led him to write an article on him, which was published in the summer of 1941 in *Common Ground*.[2]

Deciding that he did not want to pursue further education, especially since such education seemed to lead only to a teaching career, DeCapite circularized a number of small newspapers and obtained a position as reporter on the Claremont, New Hampshire *Daily Eagle*. In 1940 also, DeCapite helped Louis Adamic gather and edit material for Adamic's book *From Many Lands*. Adamic founded a short-lived quarterly *Common Ground* at about this time. DeCapite contributed the Sullivan article to it, mentioned above, and three other items in the next two years: "The Story Is Yet to be Told," an article about novels by immigrants; "War Comes to Little Italy," reportage; and "It Is Not So," a short story, which appeared again, in a slightly altered version, in DeCapite's first novel.[3]

DeCapite was earning so little on the *Daily Eagle* that his wife stayed on in New York City and worked, too, for a few months.

When DeCapite was promoted to Social Editor, she came to join him in Claremont. This assignment was so boring, however, that DeCapite and his wife decided in April, 1941 to return to New York City, where he would obtain a better position and try to sell his first novel. For a few months, he edited the Journal of the New York Hospital for Speech Disorders. In January, 1942 he became a press officer in the United Nations Information Office (called first the Inter-Allied Information Office when it was set up at the San Francisco Conference, a planning meeting for the founding of the United Nations). In addition to his work for the UN, he wrote several articles at this time about the underground presses and other underground activities in Europe and about conditions of labor in both free and occupied Europe and England.[4]

His first novel Maria, published in 1943, is the story of Italian-Americans and their problems of assimilation and is "largely autobiographical," according to DeCapite's widow.[5] In DeCapite's second novel, No Bright Banner (1944), the details of the protagonist's life follow the outlines of DeCapite's life quite closely. Paul Barone, the hero of this novel, was born in Cleveland of an Italian immigrant father and a second generation Italian mother. He attends a university in Sparta, Ohio--a faint disguise for "Athens"--and then goes to New York City with ambitions of becoming a writer. After a disillusioning sojourn in New York, he travels across the country to Chicago, bumming and working at menial jobs. In Chicago, he works as a garbage collector, and then as a reporter on a Chicago paper. No Bright Banner is a bildungsroman; by the end, Paul is sure of his own identity; he has tested the values he received from his father; Mrs. DeCapite notes, "In No Bright Banner [sic] in a way it [Paul] is himself."[6]

Another parallel between DeCapite and Barone is in literary influences. Harry R. Warfel states that

> during his college years he [DeCapite] had vague unformed ideas about a literary career. Joseph Conrad and Mark Twain were his favorite authors and he imitated them. When he discovered Sherwood Anderson, he awakened to the true possibilities of writing, and thereafter he began composing seriously.[7]

Natalie DeCapite corroborates this comment by saying that while DeCapite was still in college, he was "very impressed with Sherwood Anderson" and that his short story "Honesty" "would have been very much influenced by Winesburg, Ohio."[8]

In No Bright Banner DeCapite's hero reads boys' tales and adventure stories including Tom Sawyer and Huckleberry Finn. Later on, the reading of Sherwood Anderson's story "I Want to Know Why" leads him to read three of Anderson's novels Dark Laughter (1925), Poor White (1920), and Winesburg, Ohio (1919), which give him a taste of "the puzzling elegiac sadness of Americans, the profound uprootings of individuals."[9]

Paul also reads Sinclair Lewis' Main Street (1921), Dreiser's An American Tragedy (1925), and Hemingway's A Farewell to Arms (1929). From these books, DeCapite writes, Paul gets a picture of America "vastly different from the one in Claremont University."[10]

The first section of _No Bright Banner_ mentions that Paul's family is Italian and that his boyhood friends are Polish, but ethnicity is neglected in the rest of the book.

After a mission to England for the UNIO in 1944, DeCapite was drafted into the Army. He was put into the Field Artillery after basic training, but his temperament did not suit the kind of assembly-line work he was given to do. He passed an examination to attend Officers' Candidate School, but he decided not to leave the ranks of the enlisted men. After a brief training period for the Office of Strategic Services, he was rejected because he said he could not kill anyone even to save his own life. The Army finally found the right slot for him when it put him in charge of a news review and entertainment program in the Signal Corps. He later wrote for _Yank_ and the Army News Service in New York.

After the War, DeCapite joined the UN as a press officer. In 1947, he arranged a leave; he and his wife went to England where DeCapite helped an elderly woman edit a book, did some writing of his own, saw to the English publication of his first two novels, and then edited a pamphlet for UNESCO, which necessitated a month's stay in Paris. During this time, he and his wife toured England, Scotland, Wales, Switzerland, and parts of Italy.

In his third and last published novel _The Bennett Place_ (1948), DeCapite explores symbolically what it means to be an old-line American, the interrelatedness of persons from various ethnic and class backgrounds, and the value of integrity. The Bennett Place received mixed reviews, the usual criticism being that it was so good it was a shame that it was not better. It received the $1000 award for the best novel written by a midwesterner in 1948 from the Friends of American Writers.

From January 1949 to July 1950, DeCapite was assigned as press officer with the United Nations Commission for India and Pakistan, serving in Karachi, New Delhi, and Srinigar in Kashmir. During his eight-month assignment in Kashmir, he and his wife lived on a houseboat. One time when all his superiors were away, DeCapite handled some delicate cease-fire negotiations.[11]

DeCapite and his wife adopted two children, Philip in 1951 and Suzanne in 1954. In the summer of 1953, DeCapite and his brother Raymond visited Spain and Italy, including a visit to the DeCapite family in Rivisondoli, Abruzzi, and a visit to Ignazio Silone, whom DeCapite admired greatly.[12]

By 1958 he had become Chief of Editorial Services of the UN Department of Public Information. On a trip from Taxco to Mexico City on January 18 with the director of the UN information center in Mexico City, DeCapite was fatally injured in an automobile accident. He died in Mexico City on January 21, 1958, leaving unfinished a lengthy novel, a "personal saga" in which he tried to express the complex growth he had experienced through his sojourn in India and elsewhere.[13]

Discussion of work

DeCapite's first novel Maria (1943), dedicated "For My Mother," is the story of the adult life of a second generation Italian girl. It begins on Maria's wedding day, when she is sixteen, and ends when her daughter is sixteen, a span of about twenty-three years. It is a loose, episodic narrative of events in Maria's life. Maria is the central intelligence; her thoughts, memories, and dreams are given to the reader, but her emotions change by the author's direction rather than developing naturally, and her actions seem unmotivated.

Naturalistic novels do not have a beginning, middle, and end as nineteenth century novels did, but neither are they a series of unwrought incidents from someone's life as Maria seems to be. DeCapite chose to tell this story from Maria's point of view, but he did not manage to make her changes of mood or attitude convincing or to portray personality growth. The only growth that is indicated is Maria's feeling of gradual integration into the city. A clue to this motif is the novel's division into three parts: "Little Italy," "The South Side," and "The City."

Maria lives with her family in an Italian ghetto, speaking Italian, taking part in festas, and listening to her elders reminisce about Italy and their voyage to America. She marries an Italian immigrant, Dominic Mazzetti, who is twenty-six. Maria is not prepared for marriage. Her parents had arranged through an Italian matchmaker for her to marry. Dominic treats Maria like an object--in bed and out. His single-minded ambition to make money and his unemotional nature keep him distant from Maria and their children.

Dominic does well enough at his job for them to move from the Italian neighborhood to the south side of Cleveland, onto Literary Avenue near the mills. This south side neighborhood of Poles, Russians, and Jews is less congenial to Maria than Little Italy had been. She has no feeling for Dominic and focusses her love and attention on Paul, their first child, who is born about 1914, on Lucy, who is born when Paul is about six, and still later, on Andy, who is born right after the Crash of 1929. A flaw in DeCapite's writing is that he is vague about times and dates. For example, he says that Maria is "not yet forty" when Andy is born. If she was sixteen just prior to World War I, she would be nearer thirty or thirty-two than forty when Andy is born.

As Paul's character begins to form, he becomes more like Dominic--stubborn, silent, and selfish.[14] Maria loses interest in him even though she sometimes can feel the loneliness in him.[15] Maria loves her children while anticipating their birth and when they are infants, but she loses interest in them as they grow older. She is not capable of coping with Paul or Andy beyond infancy or adolescence. The characters Lucy and Andy are rather faceless; Lucy appears now and again with a ribbon in her hair or an offer to cook the supper; Andy barges in wanting to eat or dashes out to play ball.

When Maria and Dominic settle in the South Side, Dominic lays in a supply of Italian foods, which he sells cheaply to a few Italians. Later, he becomes a small-time bootlegger, making wine at home for Maria to sell by the glass to men who stop in after work. One of these men is Morgantonio, called "Morgan," who falls in love with Maria. He is cheery where Dominic is dour; he likes Maria's three children, gives them attention, and brings them gifts.

Dominic begins to play the stock market, borrowing money from Maria's aunt to add to his own savings. When the Crash comes, Dominic is wiped out; he loses his self-confidence as well as his money. He tries to recoup his losses, becomes panicky, and leaves Maria. He goes to Chicago and lives with his sister, Emilia.

In the third part of the novel, "The City," Maria visits Dominic (in 1932); he is a broken man, "vindictive . . . , and bitter, . . . [with the] sourness of outlook in a man who had seen his hopes and ideas crash and would not admit it to himself."[16] Maria asks him to return to her and their children, but he will not.

Maria works in a relief sewing project for a time and then marries Morgan, who has sought her out. Once or twice, in thinking of him, she has felt love and desire, but she is preoccupied on their wedding day with Paul and his opposition to her marriage. When night comes, she is distracted from Morgan's attentions by the sounds of Paul leaving home. She does not respond to Morgan then and never really cares for him afterwards. She becomes pregnant but has an abortion because she does not want Morgan's child.

Morgan leaves her, and she goes back to work. The book ends with Maria in bed after a hard day's work, dreaming of bygone days.

The only artistic shaping DeCapite gives this novel are the two wedding night scenes and the two reminiscence sequences at the beginning and the end. The book opens on Maria's wedding day with Maria recalling her sixteen years of life. It closes with the fortyish Maria dreaming of her past. On her first wedding night, Maria gazes out the window while Dominic prepares for bed; she does the same thing on her first night with Morgan. Other than these two shaping devices, the novel is formless, and the characters, for the most part, are unconvincing.

DeCapite's concern with Americanization is shown in the physical moves Maria makes. Her journey from a sheltered life in the ghetto to working in the city symbolizes her integration into the life of America. In Little Italy all the tradesmen are Italian; all interact with each other socially as well as in business. An Easter *festa* which takes place soon after Maria marries Dominic typifies this phase of her life. DeCapite describes the atmosphere as

> home to many. It was the village square in Italy again, it was song and laughter at the market place on Saturdays, it was memories made real; it was where everyone belonged, where the world and city and strange and often hostile America were shut off and forgotten.[17]

When Maria moves to the South Side, she must deal with a Russian butcher and a Polish grocer; the only neighbor she befriends is Mrs. Gelfand, the wife of a Jewish tailor. At one point, Maria goes to a large market area to shop. She travels on a street car "filled with women going to market, women jabbering in a hundred tongues."[18]

She enjoys the bustle of the market and its air of prosperity and optimism. DeCapite then gives a veritable catalog of the nationalities of the people that Maria sees:

> Chinese squeezing in and out of the crowds; flat-tongued Filopinos; gesticulating Jews and Italians; stolid, big-armed Slavs; pert, tailored Americans; red-faced Irishmen; black-haired Greeks; grinning Negroes.[19]

Maria mingles with the crowd, feeling lifted "out of herself and her four rooms. . . . for the first time in her life she felt herself a part of the city, that she was not alone, that the people about her were like herself."[20] She becomes conscious of herself and her drab clothes, feeling that she is too young to wear such clothing.

This introduction to the city is a happy one. Later, circumstances force Maria to become even better acquainted with it but not so happily. The prosperous years end when the Crash comes and Dominic leaves her. Her acquaintance with the city grows as she travels about trying to find employment. When she does find work in the relief project, it is with two hundred women. DeCapite again catalogs a melting pot:

> Widows with children, mothers whose men had left them, women with invalid husbands, elderly women with no family, young girls with mothers to support, girls alone, waiting for husbands, old and broken women, determined and hard women, frightened girls, tough

> and experienced girls, bitter and disillusioned girls, kind and patient wives, naive women working for the first time, Negro, Greek, Italian, Polish, German, Irish, English, and Russian women, stitching, sewing.[21]

After Morgan leaves, Maria again finds work sewing to support herself and her children. As she walks home from work one evening, she feels part of the workaday throng. Her assimilation into the city's life is described thus:

> Men in overalls emerged . . . . plodding silently homeward, and Maria joined them. She did this effortlessly, and she walked as one of them. Almost instinctively, during the last years since Dominic's departure and the beginning of her own struggle, she had shed her fear of the city. Without realizing it she, unlike Dominic, had experienced and achieved a sense of belonging.[22]

Maria had not tried to become an American, but she had achieved it through becoming a part of the city. She does not achieve this at the cost of family solidarity, however; at the end of the novel, Maria is still in the center of her family. She cares for her widowed mother and ancient aunt and supports her own two children who live with her.

In contrast, Dominic had tried very hard to become a part of the American system.

> He did not seem to be bothered by his being an Italian, he was not afraid of his new country. He seldom talked of the old world. In comparison with others, who were never sure, who flocked together because they seldom felt at home and never could acquire a hold in a new country, Dominic . . . believed, he knew where he was going.[23]

From the beginning of the novel, Dominic is characterized as greedy and ambitious, not letting family ties or emotions interfere with his plans or ambitions. When he begins to make money with his stock dealing, Maria contemplates him in his new suit and straw hat; she thinks

> about how handsome he is and how he looks as if he belongs in those clothes: "How more and more unlike the Italian working man she had married! . . . his body had poise--a real American business man who knew where he was going and what he was doing."[24]

They visit Maria's sister Carrie, who lives on a farm with her Italian husband, Nick. Maria compares the two men:

> [Nick] addressed himself only to Dominic. Maria thought of the early days on the hill [Little Italy], of the immigrant husbands and their old-country ways. She felt how much Dominic had changed, how, sitting there next to Nick and talking to him, how different he really was.[25]

Soon after, she realizes that he has changed in a way that hurts her. Getting deeper into stock transactions, he has entered a world that Maria does not comprehend. She is bewildered by his grasp of these transactions, recalling her father's comment about men working with their hands, as if such work were the norm. Dominic is totally caught up in his activities, blind to Maria and the children, impatient with family concerns that distract him from his schemes. His feverish activity is part of a whole social aura; he is part of the boom before the Crash.

When the Crash comes, Dominic is shattered. He tries to recoup his losses and fails but continues to live on false hopes. He has tried the American way of individualism and materialism and has failed.

Morgan, too, is a failure. He is prone to drink too much. He does not develop as a person; his experiences in World War I remain his topic of conversation ten years after the war is over. His life is a pattern of running away: he had left his parents at fourteen; he had left his Irish first wife; he leaves Maria twice.

It is difficult to work with symbolic meanings in such a plotless, unarticulated narrative as _Maria_. If there is meaning, though, it is that Americanization is a slow process, which must be carried on in company with one's family. Hard work is necessary to life; even more necessary is family solidarity. Maria has achieved a feeling of belonging to America but not at the cost of leaving her family and its values.

Those who fail in this novel are three men and one woman who leave their families. Both Dominic and Morgan left their parents at fourteen. Dominic marries an Italian girl, Maria, but he has little regard for her, their children, or her family. He even removes his nuclear family from close contact with their people. Morgan leaves his parents and both of his wives. He has an Italian name but uses an anglicized shortening of it. Bernardine, the shoemaker of Little Italy, constantly reminisces about Rivisondoli, his Italian village, but he does not marry and have a family of his own in America. When Italy is being beaten in World War I, he refuses to believe that he will never return there, quarrels with a friend about Italy, and dies.[26] Maria's oldest sister, Carrie, marries an Italian and has nine children, but she moves far away from the family; she is unhappy, discouraged, and aged beyond her years.

In DeCapite's second novel No Bright Banner, the son of immigrant parents takes center stage. Maria's son Paul was a shadowy figure who finally left home and disappeared. Paul Barone of No Bright Banner is the protagonist of this buldungsroman. His childhood, adolescence, and young manhood are told in detail. His career as student and worker is followed after he leaves his parental home. He tries to enter mainstream America, using a college education as a mobility device, but he fails. He begins to integrate his past and what he has learned in his wanderings only when he returns to his family.

Paul finds many models along the way: his father, his childhood friends, a mentor and a number of friends at college, and Cliff, a man who befriends him after his father is killed.

Paul Barone's father, his first model, gives him concepts of virility, helpfulness, curiosity, openness to life and an "emotional conviction that a companionship could be honest and good."[27] He also gives Paul a sense that one must have a direction or goal in life and not merely a job by which to make a living. He is a model of the values of an older generation, as are Cliff and Professor Whitlock later.

Paul finds models among his age-peers at three stages in his life: in his grade school years, in college, and after college. He finds both positive and negative models, i.e., he admires some boys and young men and women and wants to emulate them; some acquaintances he can neither respect nor imitate.

Cliff, an advertising man who does volunteer coaching at the YMCA, is first a positive and then a negative model. He is gregarious, lively, and generous; he introduces Paul to the pastimes and pleasures of the affluent middle class. When Paul last sees Cliff, however, he has taken to drink and is on the verge of bankruptcy, because he has not succeeded at his business even though he has succeeded at the pretence of success.

Paul's first friend at Claremont University is Steve, a miner's son of Polish descent, who had left home. He is a radical, a thinker, a seeker after truth and justice; he has the greatest influence on Paul during his first two or three years at the University. Steve's defects are that he had become bitter about life at a very early age and that he is too idealistic, too unwilling to accept the real world where change takes place slowly. He leaves college to wander the country in search of work and a place where idealism lives.

Near the end of the novel, Steve visits Paul in Chicago. He has become a heavy drinker, embittered further by his failure to find a better life for himself and a better society. He is no longer open to the good, so he will probably continue his vain search, his disappointment constantly reinforced. Steve is a disillusioned failure who lives on, letting his disillusion feed his bitterness, who has ceased to hope or to work for the betterment of himself or society.

Professor Whitlock, Steve and Paul's mentor at Claremont, is an "old American," a man whose ancestors came to America long ago.[28] He has pursued truth all his life--in thought and in people. (He mentions knowing Thorstein Veblen.) He has also pursued the history of America, exploring the geology and the flora, finding artifacts in the countryside around the university, and writing monographs on the meaning of what he discovers.

Other models at Claremont are fellow students--radicals and psuedo-radicals. For example, Brandon, who comes from a wealthy family, professes concern for the working class and the progress of radical movements, but whose interest is superficial, because it is not based on a firsthand knowledge of poverty or workers' lives. In Paul's senior year, he accompanies Brandon to New York and observes the life of Brandon's radical circle. He soon learns that there is no real activism or artistic productivity among them: they talk art as they talk radicalism.

Paul and one of these young psuedo-radicals have an affair, loving each other insofar as her masks and his insecurities allow them. When they break up, Paul works his way to Chicago to see his mother only to learn that she had died while he made his way across the country.

In this segment of the book, DeCapite involves his protagonist in several menial jobs, e.g., beanery handyman and garbage man. Paul is not satisfied with these jobs, of course, but they provide the money he needs. They also show him that self-respect can be found in hard work and that uneducated, unskilled workers can be true comrades. Paul does not continue doing this kind of work: it lacks stimulation for him, and he loathes the humiliating treatment he sometimes receives. Paul had caught pneumonia on his journey and is quite ill when he arrives at his aunt's home. She is his father's sister, an Earth Mother type. She nurses him back to health. She heals his malnourished body, and his spirit, which had been starved for reality and authenticity in persons. Steve's visit points up the contrast between the person who does not return to his family and their values and Paul who is healed by a return to a symbolic echo of the down-to-earth goodness of his father and the worth of a life that is simple and natural.

Paul becomes a reporter on a Chicago paper and learns more about the depersonalization of people--editors and policemen who have grown callous, reporters who live only for pleasure, others who live on frustrated erudition and alcohol. He learns more, also, about his own quest for personhood; he finds his identity in actions, not in ideas or movements. He realizes that for him "to build with action instead of ideas meant real work. The material was refractory and stubborn, but one could try and build slowly."[29]

At the end of the novel, World War II has begun. Paul has joined the Army and is somewhere in the Pacific. He writes a letter to Jiggs, the frustrated, alcoholic copyreader, whose basic integrity and love for learning served to make him a model for Paul;

a model and a warning, because he was a man of ideas who had not followed out his yearnings nor utilized his creative talents to the fullest. Paul writes that it is wrong to follow an ideology when one is really seeking order for his life, what one must do, rather, is hold to integrity, and the desire to be a part of healing the malaise of America.

> I believe the sickness of the world is part of our sickness. I believe the evil of acquisitiveness and expediency still is in us. . . . Our greatest job is to restore dignity to our people. . . . working to find the proper countenance for the human dream which was our promise, but which has never been fulfilled.
>
> Perhaps the end of an age is at hand, but I do not believe we have become incurably ill. . . . in my own way I love the country, and I love belonging to it. . . . And if I fight for something, I fight for what might be.and not so much for what is. . . . And I know this fight will continue when the more obvious clamor of battles is over, and I would like to be in on it.[30]

The point of view of this novel is unique in my experience. I know of no other extended prose fiction written in the second person. The use of "you" is an intrusive device; I had read several chapters before it ceased to be distracting. My assumption was that the use of second person was meant to involve the reader closely with the main character; I found it so intrusive that the opposite was true. Reviewers commented unfavorably on this device;[31] only one reviewer suggested that it lent a "feeling of intimacy."[32]

DeCapite does not deal with the change from an ethnic identity to an American identity. Paul Barone does not move from being an Italian-American to being an assimilated American. He knows his parents are Italian, but their Italian mores are not delineated nor do they associate with other Italians in Cleveland. His father is very interested in American politics, in learning, and in Paul's education.

Rose Basile Green places No Bright Banner in her "fifth phase in the development of Italian-American fiction," in which "the Italian-American 'belongs' to the national complex."[33] She says DeCapite "universalizes the character Paul who becomes adjusted only when he absorbs the philosophy of his father, Carlo, who has taught him the positive attitude necessary to find order,"[34] but one must add, he can only absorb this attitude by returning to his family.

DeCapite has universalized Paul so much, in fact, that he might be any boy of any nationality, growing up in almost any complex society. He has many models of behavior--both in an older generation and his own--but the Italian models are not Italian so much as they are honest, earthy, and full of life.

In his third novel The Bennett Place (1948), DeCapite presents a microcosm of upper class WASPs and lower class, earthy people. Each of the seven chapters has a different character as its central intelligence.[35]

The Bennett Place is the home of Katherine Bennett, an unmarried woman, the last of an old American family. Katherine and her home symbolize WASP America. The house in Sparta has big white columns in the front, and it had served as a station on the Underground Railroad. Katherine wears a blue cape (reminiscent, perhaps, of her Colonial ancestors) and lives among the portraits and heirlooms of her forebears.

Katherine is the central intelligence of the Prologue of the novel, which concerns the last hours before she shoots herself to death. Her motive for suicide is not explained by her introspection nor by the other characters who comment on her life and death, even though some of them had seen her and talked with her on the fatal day.

Katherine is seen differently by each main character in the book. She comes to have two symbolic values. To some narrators she reflects their best selves, thus helping them to see themselves "without illusion,"[36] and in some instances, to "evoke the best that was in them."[37] However, if Katherine is interpreted as a symbol of colonial or pioneer America, it is an energy-less, unproductive America, a country which has "all petered out" as one of the town men says of Katherine,[38] because Katherine herself is lacking in energy and personal dynamism. For example, she has an affair with George Mather, an effete professor at the local university, but they do not have the courage to commit themselves to each other in marriage.

It is only through comments by DeCapite himself and by his widow that this novel's central character can be understood. DeCapite is making the point in this novel that old-line America is exhausted except as an ideal of the past which can serve to inspire immigrants or lower class people, but Katherine as model and teacher was a tribute, according to Natalie DeCapite, to a teacher who had "taken an interest in" DeCapite in college. He was grateful to her for her "encouragement and kindness"; he always remembered that he "came a long way" from a "rough, uneducated background" and that his rise "was begun there" (in college).[39]

In remarks prepared for the award luncheon of the Friends of American Writers on 23 March 1949, DeCapite explained the context of The Bennett Place. These comments serve to elucidate the other symbolic value that Katherine has.

> In The Bennett Place I wrote of the end of a myth, a tradition of pioneering that has become ingrown and academic, of an innocence which no longer exists.[40]

It is the nature of symbols that they have many values, but this symbol (Katherine) has two incompatible values. The impact of this character is diffused, and thus the novel also lacks the impact it might have had as a comment upon American ideals and American society.

The lack of energy and dynamism characteristic of Katherine is also characteristic of Mather and two women of their social class. Mather, whose surname suggests that he, too, is old-line America, is the central intelligence of chapter one. His reaction to Katherine's death is presented to the reader first. Mather is upset by Katherine's death but hardly more than he is upset later by spilling tea on his newly-cleaned suit. Mather's fastidiousness and the tentativeness of his relationship with Katherine suggest that he is a latent homosexual. He is a professor but not the scholar his early life promised.

Jane Weaver, Katherine's girlhood friend, has become a rich, oversexed shrew, staying with her husband and overlooking his sexual escapades for propriety's sake and to conceal her own similar escapades. When Jane and Paul Brown's wife, another middle class woman, hear of Katherine's death, they profess to be upset, but they carry on their social lives without a halt, even relishing this grand new gossip item, looking forward to discussing it at the dance planned for the weekend. Jane is more concerned with the attention she might receive because of her early close ties with Katherine than with Katherine's wasted life or tragic end.

As DeCapite's _No Bright Banner_ was the story of an upwardly mobile boy, who came back in the end to the warmth and values of his family and class, so in _The Bennett Place_ two upwardly mobile men are portrayed. One of them finally rejects the declassifying that University education was beginning; the other has been emasculated by his successful rise. The first, Stan Havranek, an immigrant's son, has come to the University in the town where Katherine lives. After his service experience in World War II, he finds the younger students superficial and his classes unsatisfying. His link to Katherine is his work after school as a yardman at the Bennett place. The work itself and the association with Katherine are the only things that are real in his university experience, he feels. When she kills herself, he is disillusioned and leaves the university and the town.

The upward mobility provided by education in No Bright Banner is sidetracked by the Depression and by disillusion with upper-class pseudo-radicals. The hero returns to his lower class, ethnic milieu, retaining his ideal of integrity all through the novel. In The Bennett Place, on the other hand, education and upward mobility lead to loss of integrity, loss of ambition, and even finally a loss of talent. Paul Brown is a farm boy who goes to Harvard and marries the daughter of a wealthy Harvard professor. He becomes a professor at the University in Sparta, but he is a failure, because he stays with his upper-class wife, unable to pull away from the values into which she, her parents, and Harvard have indoctrinated him. At the time of his father's death, he yearns to stay at his boyhood home and enter again into the earthy life of his youth, but he cannot. He feels that "the springs of his life had ceased to nourish him the day he began to fight what was his father's integrity."[41]

Paul's wife understands neither Paul's personality nor his aspirations. When he had had a series of conversations with Katherine Bennett, on the other hand, Paul felt that he was understood. Katherine gave him insight into himself and inspiration to renew his attempts at creative writing, but Paul had allowed himself to drift away from her. When he hears of Katherine's death, he feels vaguely responsible, as if he had failed her in some way.

The symbolic meaning of Katherine vis-à-vis this vague feeling again faces the reader with a dilemma. One possible meaning is that Paul did fail Katherine Bennett by not moving ahead on his own after receiving inspiration from her. By extension, his failure may suggest the bankruptcy of the American ideals Katherine symbolizes. Either the ideals were too weak to carry Paul forward or Paul was too weak to take the ideals onto himself. Paul's acquiescence to his wife's wishes means that he has followed the American middle-class value system rather than the authentic life of his boyhood. He is a university professor, but he has lost both the talent and the intention to produce the creative work he intended in his early youth; nor is he able to produce the scholarly work required by his profession and anticipated by his wife.

Johnny O'Malley, another of the central intelligences, is the town drunk and ne'er-do-well. His section of the book is maudlin, overwritten, and tedious. He tells of his relationship with Katherine, beginning when they were children and his mother did the washing for her family. He and Katherine had loved each other, although Johnny never states this fact and it was apparently never acknowledged by either of them. Johnny had done well at his trade for a time, but service in World War I set him on the wrong road, and working for a bootlegger during Prohibition had made an alcoholic of him. Katherine supported him in these later years with gifts of money.

The possible symbolic value in this chapter is that class status had kept these two people apart, that old-line America could not accept the poor or the immigrant except in a Lady Bountiful-to-peasant relationship, and that--possibly--each of these two would have matured or been more fulfilled if they had been able to break through those barriers of class and ethnicity. This chapter is the most poorly written of the book and thus has little force.

Dr. Henry Benson, the central intelligence of the final chapter of the novel, reveals a few more details of Katherine's life and relationships, but he sheds no real light on her ambivalent character nor her still unexplained suicide.

DeCapite's style in _The Bennett Place_ is wordy, not to say mushy. His overlong and intrusive descriptions of trees, flowers, fallen leaves, and the weather are not helpful in forwarding his story, nor do they add symbolic richness.[42] The ambiguous nature of the central character and this overwriting are serious flaws in the novel.

DeCapite uses an incident in _Bennett Place_ which he had used previously in _No Bright Banner_. The description is shorter and the outcome is different, but the scene is essentially the same. George Mather recalls an incident in New York City when he had gone to a girl's room and she had read some of her writing to him and then tried to seduce him. Mather had been disgusted by the girl's sordid surroundings and had rejected her.

This incident is very like the incident in No Bright Banner which begins the sexual phase of Paul Barone's relationship with a young radical. Paul was aware of the messiness and poverty of the girl's room but was drawn to her because of her vibrancy. He allowed himself to be seduced and thus began their affair.

If my analysis of Bennett Place is correct, DeCapite endeavored to expose his views of America, but his sometimes mediocre writing and his ambivalent attitude toward his main character dilute his message. He appears to be saying that America can inspire, even though it has no vibrant life; it can raise a boy from farm to academe, but in so doing, it deprives him of earthiness and creativity. Education is a mobility device, but it is too far removed from reality: Paul Brown finishes college and comes to a dead end; Stan Havranek rejects education and leaves the university, and DeCapite gives no hint of his future. Dr. Benson has achieved contentment, but his character as friendly observer is so vague that his values are not strong enough nor his insights rich enough to explain Katherine, i.e., America, or to redeem the novel.

As Paul Brown was a writer *manqué*, so DeCapite seems to be a novelist *manqué*. He made his living for many years as a reporter and information officer, practicing many kinds of writing. He was not quite able to achieve the skills of fiction. He was not able to make the creative leap, to "make the trip" as some writers say. His three novels are based on his own life, but in none of them did DeCapite allow himself to speak directly in his own voice: he never wrote in the first person.

The three points of view that he chose are unusual. Not often do male authors write from the point of view of a woman as he did in Maria. Almost no fiction is written in the second person as No Bright Banner was. There are a few novels in which the point of view changes from one chapter to the next, but they are comparatively rare. (Faulkner's The Sound and the Fury and As I Lay Dying and Malcolm Lowry's Under the Volcano are examples of the power of this device in the hands of a skilled writer.)

To write from the point of view of the mother rather than the son in Maria allows DeCapite to try to describe the mother's feelings, even those about her son, but, as discussed above, he did not succeed in making her feelings clear or well motivated, and he did not deal with the son's feelings. To speak or write of "you" rather than "I" is a distancing device, a way of disclosing and avoiding disclosure at the same time. The shifting points of view in Bennett Place may allow the author to present many facets of Katherine Bennett, but they also allow him to decrease the attention paid to any one protagonist. Paul Brown and Stan Havranek are no more important than Mather or Johnny O'Malley or the doctor, except in the larger context the two previous novels provide.

DeCapite apparently wanted to analyze assimilation, American social structures, American ideals and values--positive and negative--and the effects on a person's values and integrity of moving upward in American society. Unfortunately, he did not have the right skills to successfully fictionalize his thoughts, feelings, and experiences. His writing is better than that of some other ethnic writers of the period, but it misses the mark. He is never quite successful in changing raw experience or keen observation into believable, stirring fiction.

Conclusion

In his published novels Michael DeCapite's view of America is that middle-class values corrupt, that real personhood lives and grows only in the working class, and that spiritual failure lurks in removing one's self from one's origins. The WASP middle class is the place of phoniness, as depicted in Cliff's wife, Jane Weaver, and Paul Brown's wife. Anyone who enters that class--by the mobility devices of education or business--will be corrupted or destroyed. He will lose his dynamism as did Dominic in *Maria*; he will lose his integrity and take to drink as did Cliff in *No Bright Banner*; he will lose his integrity, squander his talent, and become emasculated as did Paul Brown in *Bennett Place*.

Middle class women are bitches--in both the temperamental and sexual senses of the word--as Jane Weaver and Paul Brown's wife were. DeCapite's widow corroborates this reading of his novels in answer to a query:

> I think he felt that it was the women who set the values, the goals and the atmosphere in a family, and therefore they were largely responsible for perpetuating a materialistic standard in the typical middle class home. . . .
>
> I think he felt that wasting a lifetime of energy and human potential in pursuit of a two-car garage and well-kept lawns etc etc was sad. It is indeed. And corrosive, and emasculating, if you wish.[43]

The men are not manly--as illustrated by Mather and some of the pseudo-radicals in No Bright Banner. The middle class cannot even relate fully to the working class, as shown by the middle class college men who espouse radical causes but are only playing at rapport with the workers, and by Katherine Bennett, who could not acknowledge her love for the washer woman's son.

The good people are those who stay in their class, who work, and who share their goodness with others: Maria, the father and aunt in No Bright Banner, and Stan in Bennett Place. Those who retain their integrity are those who leave their upwardly mobile path and return to their people: Paul Barone and Stan Havranek.

If Katherine Bennett is a symbol of America, then America is good in its ideals or intent, but like Katherine, it has a weaker side: the failure to fulfill its ideals. Katherine is a touchstone of goodness for some of those who know her, but her own life is lacking in direction, in energy, in the ability to commit herself totally to anyone or anything.

No Bright Banner is the story of several people who are failures, but its hero has learned much about life, work, people, and himself, and at the end of the book, he has hope for a better future for America and the world. The Bennett Place is also the story of several failures; Paul Brown, for example, has let slip his opportunities to develop his writing talent and to regain his values and his integrity.

The number of persons who fail in DeCapite's novels symbolize an America which is a place where ideals are lost; where, however, the true values of hard work, integrity, and the generous sharing of material goods can be found among the unlettered but virtuous and wise immigrant generation.

It is necessary to turn to DeCapite's 1949 award speech for a fuller explanation of his attitude toward American ideals. As quoted above, he spoke of a tradition which had become "ingrown and academic" and of "a nostalgia for our protected past."[44] He spoke then of writers of his generation:

> [who,] conscious of an energy sometimes without direction, sometimes misapplied, are also seeking a new framework. I think we are becoming impatient with the negation of the 20's and the 30's, which was valid and necessary then perhaps. But we feel it is no longer legitimate. We owe much to those writers, who created a tradition in American writing and it is not easy to break away from the atmosphere they created, for so many things they said were true and are true today. But we are breaking away, I believe, and we are beginning to find in that atmosphere something facile and irresponsible. Something more is needed.
>
> We cannot escape recognition of the negative aspects of our society and our world, but we are trying to see some of the positive elements, too. We may not write enduring books in these times--we shall probably be too political and overserious and without laughter--but I believe we shall insist upon a sense of responsibility. We have a growing realization that there is today too much at stake for us to think or write as though there existed an endless luxury of time, and security. We shall insist on what could be called a recognition of human dignity. This quality of essential dignity is present everywhere here [India] where it would perhaps not be expected because it has so often been corrupted. And it has re-affirmed for me my own faith, whether I concern myself with India, or Chicago, or a small Ohio town.[45]

It is regrettable that DeCapite did not live to finish the novel he had started. The spirit of affirmation reinforced by his stay in India would have been expressed. His talent for fiction might have been realized. He applied for a Guggenheim fellowship in 1951, explaining in his application the themes of his novel in progress and his need for a year of free time for intensive work.

> In a way, this book is a development of my earlier work and experience. I feel that many of the things I have been groping for or have said in part are finally crystallizing: the responsibility of one generation to the following one; the penalty of exile, not merely exile from one's home or country, but more deeply, exile from one's sense of humanity; and the need of affirmation. On one level my book is the story of stricken idealists against the moral climate of the last fifty years; on another, it is the story of two generations, father and son; a spiritual journey described against the mind of the last generation. Its setting is America and Europe, its time is the present: but this setting is only the framework for what I hope is the simple universal story of man's need and responsibility for another and man's struggle to find his moral identity.[46]

Reading DeCapite's novels without the addition of the 1949 award speech and this Guggenheim application leaves the impression that DeCapite was disillusioned with America, that he felt its ideals had failed, had been shunted aside by materialism and the disillusioning spirit of World War II. His work for the United Nations could be seen, then, as a turning away from America, a symbolic return or commitment to Europe, and a symbolic solution to his marginal status as well.

His wife recalls that his

> disenchantment is [sic] not with America, but with what he felt was a distortion of the real ideals of our

> country. . . . The United Nations Information Office job interested him because he believed in the idea - not in America less, but the world more, and America in that world.[47]

DeCapite did not get the Guggenheim; he was not able to devote enough time to his last work. Perhaps one fragment of it can stand for DeCapite's feeling of affirmation and as an indication of what might have been: "I can only wait and listen for the dawn, for the fox drinking from the spring, for the earth to sigh and stir the fields. . . . There is the light so clear with promise."[48]

CHAPTER IV

JERRE MANGIONE--THE QUEST FOR IDENTITY

Biography

The outstanding impressions one receives from studying the life and works of Jerre Gerlando Mangione are that he has been an exemplar of the hard-working writer and that he has been ambivalent about his assimilation to America. He lived in this country and worked steadily at his craft of writing, but he spent three periods in Sicily and wrote about Sicilians--here and abroad--every time he wrote a book except for Life Sentences for Everybody (1965) and The Dream and the Deal (1972).

In his last novel Night Search (1965) he seems to have sysmbolically killed his Italian-ness and fully accepted his American-ness. Two subsequent non-fiction books, America Is Also Italian (1969) and The Dream and the Deal, indicate also that he feels being an Italian-American has a positive value, and that he owns (or reclaims) his past in a positive way.

Mangione's parents, Gaspare Mangione and Josephine (Giuseppina) Polizzi, emigrated from Sicily around the turn of the century, met and married in Rochester, New York. Jerre Gerlando, the eldest of their four children, was born there on March 20, 1909.

At the age of ten or eleven, Mangione began his writing career by ghostwriting love letters for an uncle at ten or twenty five cents a letter. He describes writing these letters in his first book Mount Allegro and apparently supplied the story to biographers, because it appears in several notices from a 1943 *Time* magazine blurb to a 1965 "Books and Authors" column.[1]

When Mangione was 17, he worked in a summer stock theatre in Rochester and appeared as a chorus boy in a revival of *Sally*. He was editor of the East High School weekly *Clarion* and a member of the Conceit Club, a small group of self-anointed literary geniuses. While working his way through Syracuse University, he founded and edited *The Chap Book*, a literary magazine, and in his senior year wrote a daily column called "Musings" for the college paper.

Mangione found a previously unknown short story by Stephen Crane in the university library and published it in *The Chap Book* in 1930. After he graduated with a B.A. in 1931, he obtained a position with *Time* magazine.

After leaving *Time*, he held a series of odd jobs and began the nearly lifelong practice of writing book reviews for major periodicals and his nearly constant practice of working at more than one writing task at a time. Between 1931 and 1945, he contributed about 75 book reviews and other articles and short stories to the New York *Herald-Tribune*, *The New Republic*, the New York *Times Book Review*, the New York *Sun*, the New York *Post*, *The Nation*, *Literary Digest*, *New Masses*, *Broun's Nutmeg*, and the *London Spectator*.

From 1934 to 1937, Mangione was a book editor for Robert McBride & Co. In 1936 he made his first journey to Italy and visited his relatives in Sicily. He had commissions to write articles about his trip; these articles appeared in *Harper's Bazaar*, *Travel*, and *The*

New Republic. Two of them, "Fontamara Revisited" and "Getting Acquainted with My Sicilian Relatives," were later revised and incorporated into the last three chapters of Mount Allegro.[2]

Mangione went to Washington, D.C. in 1937 as associate information specialist with the Resettlement Administration, moving in March to the position of National Coordinating Editor of the Federal Writers Project. In that same year, his short story "The Man With the Cracked Derby" was included in American Stuff: an Anthology of Prose and Verse by Members of the Federal Writers Project, which Mangione initiated and helped compile.

This is a slight story, told in the first person observer point of view, about a man swindling a restaurant out of a meal and getting caught. Although some of the similes are clumsy, the story shows the awareness and close observation of detail necessary to a writer.[3]

In 1939 Mangione received the first of his eight Yaddo Creative Writing Fellowships and began writing Mount Allegro during his stay at the Yaddo estate near Saratoga Springs. He resumed his government service in October 1939 as a public relations specialist for the Census Bureau and also worked on the World's Fair exhibit for the Federal Works Agency. The following June, he became an information specialist at the Department of Justice.

In July 1942 he became special assistant to the Commissioner of the U.S. Immigration and Naturalization Service in Phildelphia. He remained at the INS until 1948, becoming editor of the INS's Monthly Review in 1944. Mount Allegro was published in 1943.

In 1947 Mangione made his second trip to Sicily. In December of that year, he married Carolyn Carles, daughter of Arthur Carles, a painter in Philadelphia. They were divorced in 1952.[4]

The INS Commissioner's office moved from Philadelphia to Washington in 1948, but Mangione remained in Philadelphia and worked in advertising and public relations there and in New York City until 1961. In 1948, Mangione's second novel The Ship and the Flame was published. In 1950, Mangione and Edward Peeples wrote a play script from Mount Allegro which was staged by the Experimental Theatre of Philadelphia. Reunion in Sicily, a book about Mangione's 1947 trip to Sicily, was published in the same year.

Mangione married Patricia Anthony, an artist, on February 18, 1957.

A new career began for Mangione when he became Director of freshman composition courses in the Department of English at the University of Pennsylvania in 1961, but he continued to write. He became director of the University's writing program in 1965.

Mangione took a leave from the University in 1965 to accept a Fulbright research grant in Sicily. While he researched and recorded the life and works of Danilo Dolci, his wife painted scenes of Sicily, which were exhibited in Sicily and later in New York. In the fall of that year, he had two books published: his third novel Night Search and a slim book of satirical sketches Life Sentences for Everybody.

His research on Dolci and the story of his six-month stay in Sicily was published in 1968 as A Passion for Sicilians: the World Around Danilo Dolci. Also in that year he received a Rockefeller

Foundation research grant and served as a judge for the fiction award of the National Book Awards. The following year, his America Is Also Italian launched G.P. Putnam's Sons' juvenile series about ethnic groups in America.

The Republic of Italy recognized Mangione's literary contributions by making him a Knight Commander of the order of the Star of Italian Solidarity in November 1971.[5]

In 1972, Mount Allegro was reprinted for the third time, A Passion for Sicilians was republished in a paperback edition under the title The World Around Danilo Dolci, and a new book The Dream and the Deal: The Federal Writers' Project 1935-1943 was published.

Mangione outlined his literary career in a "Statement of Literary Purposes" he wrote in 1972 for a British biographical directory:

> As a writer I am motivated by the need to understand myself and the world around me. This need was first nourished by the circumstances of being born and raised among Sicilian-born relatives in an urban American environment. That experience, which is the substance of my first book, MOUNT ALLEGRO, accentuated for me the sharp contrast between the philosophical values of the old world and those of the new. It also succeeded in casting me in the role of the outsider who, belonging to neither world, tries to create his own world by the writing of fiction. Two of my novels, THE SHIP AND THE FLAME and NIGHT SEARCH . . . are efforts in that direction, and for that reason

may be more truly autobiographical than the three books I have written in the first person, namely MOUNT ALLEGRO, REUNION IN SICILY, and A PASSION FOR SICILIANS. Although MOUNT ALLEGRO is somewhat fictional in content, it is a basic part of this trilogy which extends over a span of fifty years and deals largely with my public identity as a Sicilian American observing the people and places he knows best.[6]

Discussion of work

Mangione's first novel Mount Allegro (1942) begins with a young sister of the protagonist saying, "When I grow up I want to be an American"[7] and then the comments of the other children as to what that remark might mean. From their father, teachers, and some neighborhood boys of different ethnic backgrounds, these children learn that they are not Americans or even Italians, as they had thought, but Sicilians, who may become Americans in time.

Mangione's protagonist, Gerlando, questions this matter of nationality and tells how teachers in the public school assumed that children with Italian names would be talented in music, drawing, and the Romance languages. The Americanizatin theme is then dropped not to be overtly dealt with again until the last fourth of the book.

The chapters between one and twelve concern Gerlando's home life and social events among his extended family and Sicilian neighbors. Some of the chapter headings are indicative of Mangione's themes: "Family Party," "God and the Sicilians," "Evil Eye," and "Sicilian Virgin."

The purpose of these anecdotal chapters comes clear only in the last two chapters of the book when Gerlando as a young man goes to visit his relatives in Sicily. Chapter 12 "New Bread, Old Wine" is a transition between the description of Sicilian-American life and the comparison with life in Sicily. Mangione's protagonist, Gerlando, ponders the notion of Americanization, because feeling the example of his relatives is too strong. Gerlando says:

> At eighteen I left my Sicilian relatives. Living among them, I had the sense that though I was born in America I was not really an American. I decided to become a part of the outer American world; perhaps in that way I could rid myself of the feeling that I was more Sicilian than American. . . . The influence of my relatives was stronger than that of my teachers, stronger than all the movies I had seen and the books I had read.[8]

Gerlando had had after school and summer jobs, which had given him glimpses of America outside his ethnic milieu. At eighteen he went to college and after that to New York to work as a writer; Mangione's protagonist thus followed the pattern of Mangione's own life. Gerlando never lived in Rochester again, but he gained understanding of his relatives and his heritage by gaining understanding of other Americans whom he met. He expresses his feelings in this way:

> I got caught in the whirlpool of American life.
>
> I began to know America and feel like an American, and gradually to learn that America did not differ so much from the street I grew up on. The people I met--and I met many--were much like those I had known in Rochester. But now I could see them more distinctly and fit them into the pattern that was America. At the same time, I learned to see my relatives more objectively, and, although I still retained my childhood resentment for some of their habits and attitudes, for the first time in my life I began to appreciate their warmth and their talent for living.[9]

Marcus Lee Hansen has said that what the son wants to forget, the grandson wants to remember. In the case of Mangione's hero, however, it was the son who wanted to remember; i.e., to learn about his ancestors and his heritage. Even though his career separated him from his family, he began to appreciate them more as the years went by.

> My bond with them grew stronger through the years. . . . The less desire I had to cut myself off from them. The memory of my life in Rochester gave me a root feeling, a sense of the past which I seemed to need to make the present more bearable. I found myself admiring my relatives for some of the same qualities I had once disliked, and wishing I could share their warm and easy acceptance of life.

> Like a man who becomes interested in the old wine he has been drinking, I tried to trace their origins.[10]

Gerlando read travel books, history books, and books about America as a melting pot. He questioned himself as to the value of Sicilians to America, of reasons why changes should or might come into the lives of Sicilians in this country, and of reasons why such changes might not come. He decided that he needed to go to Sicily and see the country and his people first hand.

Through the eyes of Gerlando, Mangione compares and contrasts the mores and attitudes of the American Sicilians with the customs and attitudes of Sicilians on their native island.

Until Gerlando went to Sicily, he had thought that American Sicilians had not changes their customs, attitudes, or the Sicilian language of their youth. But Gerlando learns that his relatives had adopted many American customs, abandoned some Sicilian customs, and allowed many American words to creep into their native tongue.

Gerlando's visit occurs at the height of Mussolini's power; Mangione portrays the Sicilians as suspicious of each other, secretive, and not quite able to be wholeheartedly fun-loving and free in each other's presence.[11] American Sicilians were more Sicilian, in a sense, because they were able to maintain their exuberance better than their relatives under the shadow of fascism. The journey of the protagonist away from his Sicilian ethnic milieu is a journey back to Mount Allegro in the end.

Mount Allegro is full of humor and human foibles. Evil and

good are portrayed; whichever triumphs, however, it is wit and wisdom and knowledge of human nature that allow it to triumph. One difference between Mount Allegro and Pietro DiDonato's Christ in Concrete, another novel of Italians in America, is that DiDonato concentrates on a nuclear family and its hardships, giving very little attention to anyone outside the Italian ethnic group and almost none to what it means to be an American.

Mount Allegro details only the sunnier side of life, possibly for the artistic purpose of pointing up contrasts with Sicily, but it has a serious purpose under the humorous attitude: to help the reader vicariously experience the life of these exuberant Sicilians, to show their warmth and their art of living.

In Current Biography (1943), Mangione discussed his purposes in writing about the Sicilian-Americans:

> They seemed so much gayer and more exciting than the people I met in the world outside their world, . . . Also, I was tired of sociological books about the foreign-born and of novels about them that strove for dramatic effects at the expense of everything else. . . . I hope that my book will not only contribute to a better understanding of Sicilians and, to some degree, of Italians, but will also serve as an impetus to those creative writers who are familiar with similar material about other minority groups.[12]

At the same time, Mangione seems to be attempting in this first novel to answer the question he posed through the children's responses to Giustina's "When I grow up I want to be an American." Mangione's ambivalence was felt by Isaac Rosenfeld in reviewing Mount Allegro for The New Republic. Toward the end of his review, he states:

> Mangione remains essentially a man of two cultures. Thus, when he pays a visit to Sicily, . . . he gains final insight, through his own alienation, into the nature of his people.[13]

If my analysis of his work is correct, Mangione did not complete his answer until about twenty years had passed.

In The Ship and the Flame (1948) the protagonist is a Sicilian university professor who is fleeing from political arrest as are several other characters in this novel of World War II. It is not concerned with Americans or Americanization; the central emphasis of the story is commitment rather than identity. The setting of a ship at sea--between Europe and America--may symbolize that Mangione still had not decided which heritage was more truly his. The thrust of the novel, though, is that a man must live out his principles, be a man, even though he may be in limbo between one country and another.

The character of Mangione's hero, Stiano Argento, develops as the people he interacts with and the incidents which occur call forth his potentialities. He changes because the necessity to act in behalf of others is thrust upon him.

Stiano renews his friendship with an old schoolmate, Josef Renner, who is on the same ship. They renew also their old argument about good men and the necessity to actively combat evil. Even though Stiano had been aware of evil and had had a negative opinion of the politics of his country, his feeling had always been that a life of study and teaching precluded activism. He had finally committed a political act, however, and had had to flee his home in Sicily. Renner had always been an activist--not only quarreling with evil but combatting it.

When a German submarine stops their ship in mid-ocean and Renner is ordered to board it, he know there is no escape. Feeling that he had done as much as possible for freedom by his journalistic activities and political agitation, he kills himself rather than face imprisonment and torture in German-occupied Europe.

Stiano is forced to take over some of Renner's role and put the ideals he had once again heard from his old friend into practice. When the ship arrives in Mexico and the passengers discover their Mexican visas are fraudulent, Stiano and two other passengers are elected to speak for all of them.

The Portuguese captain cannot, or will not, land them in Mexico even to travel across it to other countries for which they have entrance visas. Stiano and the others try to negotiatate with the captain to take them to a neutral country rather than back to Casablanca and danger.

Later, when the ship docks in the United States to refuel and replenish its supplies, Stiano has become bold enough to take on negotiations with American social workers.

The "ship" in the novel's title may symbolize a world in

which people must act to save themselves or to improve their lot; a world in which some have gifts which must be used for the benefit of others who are less aware, less concerned, or less powerful.

The journey across the ocean is also Stiano's psychological journey from passive to active. He develops his potential for service, his organizational abilities, and leadership qualities which he did not know he had.

As a physical journey often symbolizes a psychological journey, so a flame often symbolizes passion. The "flame" of the book's title may symbolize two things: Stiano's passionate attraction to a Polish woman, Tereza Lenska, and her passionate nature. Tereza, Renner's mistress, encourages and aids both Renner and Stiano in their efforts to help their fellow passengers, sometimes by accepting, or seeming to accept, the captain's amorous advances. Her character and her sacrificial acts are emotional parallels to Renner's philosophy and activism.

The epigraph to _The Ship and the Flame_ is a saying of Justice Oliver Wendell Holmes, "Man is born to act. To act is to affirm the worth of an end, and to affirm the worth of an end is to create an ideal." Mangione's concern is in portraying the metamorphosis of a good man who had done nothing and let evil flourish into a man who acted, who affirmed the worth of freedom and truth, and who began to help create ideals.

Mangione's creation, Stiano, always an idealist, chooses to

be a man of action even though he is suspended between two countries, but belonging to neither. He has loved Tereza Lenska, the passionate woman of action, and learned from her, but he is still dutiful enough to stay with his old-fashioned Sicilian wife.

It may be possible that at the time Mangione created this fictional world, he was manifesting a choice to be a man who affirmed his ideals, even though he might feel he was an outsider belonging to neither the old world nor the new.

<u>Reunion in Sicily</u> (1950), Mangione's third book, is similar to <u>Mount Allegro</u> in format and style, but the narration of Mangione's second visit to Sicily is not fictionized. In it, the observer and narrator is Jerre Mangione himself; the events of his episodic narrative are held together by his presence.

Since the earlier visit, his relatives have grown older, of course; the adolescents are now married or finishing their education. Some of the older people now repudiate their previous admiration for Mussolini, but others attempt to justify what was good in Fascist Italy in order to justify their own former approval.

Mangione knew that D.H. Lawrence had lived in Sicily and written about it. He took this opportunity to visit the house where Lawrence and his wife Frieda had lived and learn from the owner of the house what he could recollect of the Lawrences. When Mangione writes of this incident in <u>Reunion in Sicily</u>, he contrasts Lawrence's feelings about Sicily with his own.

Lawrence, he writes, was "both attracted and repelled" even though he knew the Sicilians well from living in Sicily and from translating the work of the Sicilian novelist Verga. Lawrence's repulsion is attributed by Mangione to innate qualities. Mangione writes, "Perhaps the explanation is that, biologically at least, he was never able to overcome his Anglo-Saxon temperament."[14]

A few paragraphs further, Mangione seems to contradict this attribution of a person's attitudes toward Sicily to biology. Perhaps he wants his own appreciation for that island and its people to be shared by many and feels he must not attribute such liking only to his genes. He comments:

> Of all the foreigners who have lived in Sicily, Lawrence interested me most, partly because he was so articulate and honest, partly because I knew enough about the Anglo-Saxon mentality to see Sicilians through his eyes. But since my heritage was Sicilian I could also see his unconscious distortions, the false impressions and all the rest of the obstacles that prevented him from finding a "kinship" among them. My thinking about Lawrence made me realize, as I never had before, that my own feeling of kinship toward the Sicilians went beyond ancestral ties. And I became convinced that, regardless of nationality, anyone who approached the Sicilians sympathetically and was not too blinded by their past could find in them a warmth and wisdom more rewarding than all the ruins on the island.[15]

This musing is another indication of Mangione's ambivalent feelings about his identity. He acknowledges the kinship of heredity, but he seems to need to justify his deep feelings on another basis.

Mangione's third novel Night Search and a small book Life Sentences for Everybody were published in October and November 1965. The short pieces in Life Sentences were called "satiric fables"[16] and described as "satiric and pungent."[17] Mangione comments that they "were inspired by the challenge of telling a story within the confines of a single sentence."[18]

Night Search is a mystery-adventure cum bildungsroman, and in its intensity is unlike any of Mangione's other work. It cannot be read simply as a mystery-adventure, because underlying the protagonist's quest for the murderer of his father is a quest for resolution of his own identity problem.

This second quest contributes to the intensity as does a further complication in the story: details about the protagonist's dead wife and their relationship. This relationship is not necessary to the solution of the mystery, and it seems not clearly necessary to the identity quest.

The protagonist's name is Michael Malory, but Malory is his stepfather's name. Michael's real father was Paolo Polizzi, an Italian immigrant active in politics and journalism, a man of great warmth, exuberance, and energy, who had been assassinated some years before the time in Michael's life covered in the novel. Mangione has stated that "the writing of the novel [Night Search] had been stimulated by the memory of a prominent labor leader I knew personally who was murdered by an unknown killer."[19]

The description of the character Paolo Polizzi, including his size, his penchant for breaking up Fascist meetings (one of which Michael attended with him as an adolescent), and the fact that he was gunned down in the street by an unknown assailant parallels the description of Carlo Tresca whom Mangione calls "the best known of the Italian-American radicals" in America Is Also Italian:

> the dynamic publisher of a New York newspaper issued in Italian, Il Martello (The Hammer). When Italy succumbed to the Fascist dictatorship of Benito Mussolini, Tresca began to devote most of his efforts to fighting Fascist propaganda in America. His weapons were his newspaper, his talent as an orator, and his big fists. In the thirties, when Mussolini was at the height of his power, Tresca and his friends broke up many a meeting of Fascist sympathizers in New York City. . . .
>
> On a wintry evening in January, 1943, Tresca was shot in the back by an unknown assassin.[20]

When Night Search opens, Michael Malory is about 35; he has just quit his job as a public relations man and is seeking employment in Boston. He had been informed that his wife, Nina, confined in a mental institution, had committed suicide. He goes for a few days to Cape Cod, where two important events occur: he overhears a conversation that starts him on the trail of his father's murderer, and he meets a young woman, Lucy Hawthorne, to whom he is immediately attracted.

The story is complex on the level of mystery-adventure, but it is complicated further by Michael's personal growth and mental turmoil. While he recalls and re-evaluates his relationship with Paolo Polizzi, he is also recalling and re-evaluating his relationship with Nina. In Mangione's 1969 speech about the hidden depths of the writer's unconscious, he said the suicide of Nina emphasizes Michael's sense of failure.[21]

To summarize the outcome of the three levels of the novel briefly--on the mystery-adventure level, Michael finds and forgives the man, Vincenzo Russo, who had suffered the guilt of Paolo's murder for many years. Russo had not pulled the trigger and killed Paolo, but he had tipped off the gangster enemies of Paolo who then shot him down. Russo had wanted Paolo killed, because he believed that Paolo had dishonored his sister, Lisa.

Michael discovers that Lisa had also been guilt-ridden through the years, because she had suspected what her brother had done and was afraid to reveal to him that it was not Paolo who had gotten her pregnant. Michael's investigation and revelations help this brother and sister to emerge from their guilt feelings and their clouded relationship and to begin to live more freely and openly.

On the bildungsroman level, Michael frees himself from his attachment to Paolo through this investigation. He had met his father a few times in his adolescence and young manhood, but he knew him only as a flamboyant public figure. As Michael meets and questions the people who had known Paolo, he begins to understand Paolo as a human being, reduced in size from the godlike public figure of Michael's earlier impressions and fantasies. When Michael realizes his own identity by breaking the hold that Paolo had on him, he is free to be himself, no longer bound either to Paolo by the attraction of mystery nor to his stepfather William Malory by gratitude. He is a free, mature man, who no longer has to think of himself as the unknown son of a great man.

In answer to my query, Mangione summarized Michael's quest thus:

> Michael was not only searching for his identity but also for something that would give his life meaning. The search for the murderer was part of that quest but, of course, it was also a quest for reality. In the end, he knows the painful truth about his father - and the futility of finding the assassin - yet he is able to survive. And without succumbing to violence. . . . Accepting the truth about one's own father, understanding it, is only a small part of the quest for reality and self-identity.[22]

Nina's death freed Michael from her. Throughout the narrative, he slowly realizes what she had done to his personality and how his more gentle, loving nature had been injured by her need for too-passionate acts.

As Mangione commented to me on this aspect of the novel:

> Nina is a necessary character in the book because she represents that part of Michael's life which was an escape from reality - and from himself, of course. . . . I would agree with you that as long as he became involved with a Nina or any

other sexpot he would be postponing his confrontation with reality - or, as you put it, with "his true self."[23]

A symbolic analysis of <u>Night Search</u> in relation to Mangione's life suggests the following. Mangione wrote of his own search for American identity in this novel. He--through his protagonist Michael Malory--chose America. There are correspondences between <u>Night Search</u> and Mangione's life. One is that both Michael and Mangione were public relations men. Another is that in 1937 Mangione used the pseudonym "Mario Michele" when he wrote about his visit to Sicily. "Michele" is the Italian equivalent of Michael, so Mangione had used the name Michael for himself.[24]

Mangione's mother's maiden name was Polizzi, so Paolo Polizzi may symbolize Mangione's ties to the old country, to his parents' nationality.

William Malory, Michael's stepfather, is a shadowy figure, old and not the least flamboyant. He could symbolize America, which gives the name "American" to the children of the foreign-born, as Malory gave his name to Michael, but remains remote or impersonal to some of them.

Lucy Hawthorne also probably represents America; her last name is an obvious reference to old-line America and its Puritan heritage. She has lost her father; it is possible that she represents, also, the fatherless, Adamic American of the Turner, Handlin, R.W.B. Lewis tradition, which Michael joins at the end of the novel.

Michael's mother was a radical in her youth; hence the affair with Paolo Polizzi. She became a conservative in her middle years: hence the marriage with Malory. She may also be a foil for Michael; her movement from a foreign-born lover to an American husband serves to underscore the story of Michael's detachment from his foreign-born father and his movement to autonomy as an American.

Mangione may have summed up both Michael's quest and his own in the epigraph from Hamlet he placed on the title page of Night Search: "I am thy father's spirit; Doomed for a certain term to walk the night. . . ." Hamlet does not have to seek his father's spirit, but in Mangione's novel, the father's true spirit must be searched for, and the son (who in a sense is also the father's spirit) fulfills his destiny to search in his own dark night of the soul and lay to rest this ghost of divided identity within himself.

In 1969 Mangione noted that in Night Search his "psyche was able to achieve a synthesis which had evaded his consciousness."[25] In answer to a query, "How much of Michael's quest was your own?" Mangione replied, "As for Michael's quest being my own, isn't it the quest of every human being?"[26]

Mangione's next book A Passion for Sicilians: The World Around Danilo Dolci (1968) is another reunion in Sicily for Mangione, but this time the focus is not on him and his family but on the life and work of Danilo Dolci and on what Dolci can mean to Sicily. Because of his ties with the Sicilians and his previous visits, Mangione is able to bring an insider's perspective to his evaluations of Dolci and some others who are similarly engaged but less well known.

Mangione presents both the good and the bad of Dolci's personality, sometimes as manifested by himself, sometimes as depicted by those who had worked for him and then left his group. Dolci emerges as a fine and wise man, neither a saint nor a prophet, whose work of helping Sicily goes more slowly than he would like because he attempts to work with the Sicilian people to modernize their government and their technology.

The style of this book is almost casual; Mangione narrates his stay in Sicily, individual episodes with Dolci, and interviews with other Sicilians almost in a day-to-day account. There must be more artistic selection and shaping than is obvious.

For example, Mangione narrates a discussion with a Sicilian woman about the changes taking place in Sicilian ways in America. He speaks to her of the freedom that Sicilian girls enjoy in America, the end of the despotism of the Sicilian father, and the freedom young people have to choose their own spouses or to live far from their parents. Finally, he reports this part of the dialogue:

> "Sicilian culture, as you know it here," I said, "is vanishing in the United States. In a couple of generations there won't be any trace of it, except for a few Sicilian names that Americans have trouble spelling."
>
> "Is all that desirable?" Paola asked. "If people lose their sense of being Sicilian, they will lose the qualities that make Sicilians so attractive. They will become like everyone else, like the Italians who live in an industrialized

society . . ."

We were interrupted by the arrival of her Swedish guest.[27]

This conversation is never resumed nor the thoughts ever finished. It appears that Mangione sees the Sicilians as being Americanized and that there is both good and bad in the process, but he cannot yet resolve whether it is good or bad ultimately. An artist does not leave a conversation unfinished or a thought unconcluded unless he wants them to be.

G. P. Putnam's Sons chose Mangione to write the first book in their new series of juveniles about immigrant groups "who left their native lands to join the mainstream of American life" as the dust jacket announces. In <u>America Is Also Italian</u> (1969) Mangione presents some facts and figures about the great wave of Italian immigration as well as some earlier history. He also includes brief biographies of famous Italian-Americans and lists of successful singers, sports figures, politicians, actors, writers, and others, which are reminiscent of similar lists in the filio-pietistic books of an earlier time.

Mangione has done his homework in Handlin, Higham, and Glazer and Moynihan, accepting in fact, Handlin's term "uprooted" without reconciling it with the close-knit extended families and the neighborliness he himself depicted so well in <u>Mount Allegro</u> and his books about Sicily. <u>America Is Also Italian</u> was not intended as an in-depth study--historically or sociologically. It is a positive view of Italians in America; it reveals that an Italian is assimilable.

Mangione's latest book The Dream and the Deal: The Federal Writers' Project 1935-1943 is a social history of a unique moment, a unique project in America's history. It is well-researched history by a person who was part of the events he now writes about. It is not, perhaps, the definitive history, but it is a valuable document, nevertheless. Mangione narrates anecdotes of events in which he played a part, but he does not treat ethnicity, either his own or others'.

What can be said about these two books, in the broad sweep of Mangione's writing life, is that they indicate that he has accepted his American-ness. These indicate a reclaiming or "owning" of his past. If he made the choice--expressed symbolically in Night Search--that he is an American, he "owns" his American-ness by delving into the history of his people in America and his own history as part of the Federal Writers Project.

Conclusion

Nearly all of his life, Mangione has worked simultaneously at several writing tasks. He has written about himself and about his Sicilian people, here and in Sicily, in nearly all of his books, fiction and non-fiction. Olga Peragallo indicated in 1949 that Mangione wrote to explain the Italians to Americans. She quoted him as saying:

> Although . . . Italian-Americans are a definite part of America few people know very much about them. . . . They

> [Americans] like their Italian neighbors well enough, but they have little conception about what kind of people they are, what sort of lives they lead, what they think about American women and American religion, and what they do about American women and American religion.[28]

She continues to discuss his ideas about Americanization, paraphrasing his belief "that the first generation can never be wholly Americanized. . . . The second generation is the fusing of the two civilizations, and the third is the accomplished finished product."[29]

As a second generation Sicilian himself, Mangione typifies the fusion of the two civilizations; as a writer he has been able to live out this fusion in ways that many other members of his generation could not. He has traveled back and forth between the two countries of his allegiance, integrating not only the reminiscences of his parents and relatives in Mount Allegro but also being a part of Sicily on his extended visits there.

He has expressed his ambivalence in his writings: sometimes in his own person and sometimes in the guise of characters he invented to symbolize rather than state his growth and feelings.

In America Is Also Italian, his latest effort to explain Italians to Americans, Mangione says

> America has influenced the Italian immigrants with its youth and vigor, while the Italians have sown throughout the nation the seeds of their warmth and wisdom.[30]

What is intriguing here is the phrase "warmth and wisdom," exactly the same words used 29 years earlier in Reunion in Sicily to describe the Sicilians in Sicily.

In writing of the Italians of the pre-World War II period in American Is Also Italian, Mangione says that the children of Italian immigrants had

> problems of adjustment . . . often more painful than those of their parents. Most of all, they wanted to be considered Americans. But as children they had been obliged to live two lives: to be Italians at home . . . and to be Americans with their playmates and at school.[31]

Here, Mangione harks back to the ambivalence of his childhood, to the "unhealed psychic wounds" that authors write about in symbols.[32]

He is currently at work on two books--a novel and a non-fiction book with the tentative title An Ethnic at Large about "his search for American values after leaving Mount Allegro."[33] His quest for identity was largely resolved in the symbolic Michael of Night Search, but the ambivalence which makes such a quest necessary is apparently never quite forgotten.

CHAPTER V

BEN FIELD--IDENTITY CHOICE DEFERRED BY GROUP MEMBERSHIP

Biography

Ben Field is a marvelously refreshing writer; his stories and novels have movement, earthiness, and a feel of authenticity. His characters are individuals: some dour, some humorous, some anecdotal, some wise, many earthy and bawdy in speech and action, but all lively and believable. His locales--farm or machine shop, village or large city--are authentic because Field writes of places and occupations he knows. He has been a farmer, logger, machinist, and teacher as well as writer.

"Ben Field" is a pseudonym for Moses Bragin. He was born on October 15, 1901 in Russia and came to America at the age of four. He was raised in Brooklyn and still lives there with his wife, Jeannette. They have one son, Joe. Of his early life, he writes,

> Ours was a bookish family. Immigrant friends of my parents, [sic] often stayed with us as lodgers upon their arrival in the United States. They were of the Russian Jewish intelligentsia, who were familiar with Yiddish, Hebrew, and Russian classics. Gorky, Tolstoi, Sholom Aleichem, Peretz [Hirschbein], Mendele Mochersforim, [Chaim Nachman] Bialik - these writers and many others were read and discussed by them at their weekly gatherings. I became an avid reader, an eager listener, and a contributor to the Circle. My first story was read to these men and women. . . .
>
> I was a shy and sheltered stringbean at the age of fifteen, when I began to write. I was no athlete, and perhaps that was the vent through which the turbulence deep within me had its outlet.[1]

Ben Field attended public school in Brooklyn, received a B.A. from the College of the City of New York and an M.A. from Columbia. While still in school, he worked on a dairy farm in upper New York State. He also earned a New York elementary teaching certificate but taught only in a Yeshiva school in the English department. He taught less than twenty hours a week and he had July and August free, so even after he began teaching, he took opportunities to work on farms and travel through the country.

> I came to love farming during World War I when I worked on a dairy farm in New York State and on a tobacco-dairy farm in Connecticut. Tired of teaching and the reading of books, a Tolstoyan of a sort and a premature Hippy [sic], I turned to working with my hands as a machinist and a logger.[2]

It was probably the influence of his father's friends that turned Field to writing.[3] In 1930 he began publishing stories about Jewish family life, for the most part. One of his first stories, "A Japanese Kimono," appeared in an anthology _Copy 1930_, which was a compilation of the published work of students in special writing courses in the Columbia University Extension Division. The autobiographical blurb Field wrote for this book ends with the statement, "My two greatest ambitions are to write a fine story and plow a field without having to 'cut and cover.'"[4]

He wrote short stories, poems, and reportorial sketches at this time, which were printed in the _New Masses_, the _Daily Worker_, _Partisan Review_, _Poetry_, and some little magazines. A short story "Cow," printed in _The Hound & Horn_ in 1931, is narrated by Mose, a young man who explains that he is "working on the farm to get some material for some farm stories."[5] "Cow" combines Field's two milieux; it is the story of a Jewish city man and the influence he exerts on the people he meets while working on a farm. This story and "The Grasshopper is Stirring," a reportorial sketch for the New Masses, were reprinted in Proletarian Literature in the U.S.

Field and his wife traveled across America, and their trip resulted in "Journal of a Tour of America" and "Sentimental Cross-Country" which were printed in 1932. In 1932, also, Field writes

> I began writing under the name Ben Field. The chief reason for the switch was my turning to the farm as my main source of material. My turning to the Left was also a reason for operating under another flag, so to speak - Ben Field. . . . "The Grasshopper is Stirring" in Proletarian Literature [sic] is farm reportage of Ben Field moving left.[6]

About this same time, Field went to Russia to study collective farms.[7] Although Field was neither a Communist nor a Marxist, he has been a farm organizer and a shop steward and is still a leftist and a progressive. He believes Marx to be a great, seminal thinker and approves of many causes which the Communists espouse.[8] The Daily Worker, the New Masses, and International Publishers were, as he writes,

> the vehicles which carried my freight to thousands of readers on the Left, (Communists, Marxists, Socialists,) and workers and farmers who were not members of any radical group but, as progressives, found fiction and reportage about their lives interesting; the writing of a number of us at that time, members of the John Reed Club, held a mirror up to them.[9]

International Publishers brought out The Cock's Funeral, a collection of thirteen of Field's short stories, in 1937, including the title story, "Cow," "The Sheep Dip," based on his experiences on a farm in Michigan in 1933, and three stories about Lew Benson and his family, based on the life and character of a militant leader in the Farmer's Protective Association in Pennsylvania, whom Field knew.[10]

Field left the teaching profession in 1940 and began working in a machine shop. His first novel The Outside Leaf was published in 1943. In 1946 his second novel Piper Tompkins, which is about a machinist, was published and a short story "An Answer for My Uncle" was reprinted in Accent Anthology: selections from Accent, a quarterly of new literature, 1940-1945.[11]

Work as a logger in the Upper Delaware River Valley of Pennsylvania and New York contributed to the writing of Field's third novel The Last Freshet (1948). His short story "A Lesson" was also reprinted that year in Joseph Gaer's anthology Our Lives, American Labor Stories. Field was active in the American Labor Party about this time, working on short stories and three novelettes in his free time. Only an occasional story, article, or book review was published, however.

He considered The Last Freshet a failure; he reexamined his work, as he says, "to try to learn what was amiss, and to get to work to correct it. So I became a locust and went underground."[12] He returned to teaching in 1953 as an instructor in social studies and English in private preparatory schools. In 1970 he retired from teaching. The first novel of a trilogy appeared in 1971.

Jacob's Son contains many elements of Field's earlier work but implies a different Weltanschauung. He is currently at work on the second novel and has outlined the third. An article on Bialik, an important influence on the protagonist of the trilogy, appeared in Jewish Currents in May, 1973 in commemoration of Bialik's centenary.[13]

Field is a writer who observed firsthand the plight of workers of the lowest class and who felt an obligation to aid those workers by publicizing that plight and ways their difficulties should be overcome. His four novels are about workers. The first and last of them are about Russian Jews, but not until Jacob's Son did Field deal with the Americanization of immigrants and their children. The adolescent growth theme is common to all of his novels, but only in the last is the father dead and the young protagonist consciously free from a clinging heritage. It seems, then, that Field was concerned with personal autonomy all of his life, but only in his late years did he, like Mangione, reconcile an attachment to the past with freedom from it.

Themes that appear again and again in Field's work are personal growth and freedom, discipline, and responsibility. He was concerned also with the relationship of men and women. His protagonists are men, but the women in his novels are not subservient; the best of them are as autonomous as men. Until his middle years, Field was an activist and believed in organizations of workers, on the farm as well as in the factory. He also believed in the value of work and the strength of the person.

Discussion of work

Ben Field's style of writing is forceful; he uses many short, declarative sentences, action verbs, and powerful nouns. His people don't "turn around," they "hurl around." His working men don't have hands; they have fists, whether they are holding a scythe or a pen. When two farm hands in "In the Grass" ask for work, standing on a porch at night, Field writes that the farmer "combed them suspiciously with his flashlight,"[14] thus creating a vivid picture in few words.

Most of his short stories, written between 1930 and 1940, describe the rural poor, family farmers or itinerant farm hands. Many of these stories deal with rebellion: the sudden resistance of one or two persons, plans for defiant action, or the consequences of such actions. He wrote of families and family solidarity, of families helping other families, of boys and girls taking on responsibility or learning lessons about how people are exploited.

Two of Field's short stories, "Cow" and "An Answer for My Uncle," foreshadow much of his later work. "Cow" (1931) is a powerful story of a Jewish carpenter who works on a farm for a brief time and then is killed. The man is known only as "Cow." His self-discipline and his concern for workers become thematic in Field's work; Cow himself is the prototype of two characters who appear later in novels. Cow is a very large man, strong and very adept at his work. He performs prodigious feats of strength and endurance.[15]

Cow's ideology includes self-discipline, integrity, the responsibility of the strong for the weak, and a belief in action against exploitation of workers. Cow is fatally injured when he jumps down from a hayloft onto a pitchfork deliberately left in a dangerous position by the foreman who hates and fears him.

The end of the story is symbolic. After Cow's death, the narrator quits his job on the farm. As he is driven to the train station by the farm owner, he describes what he sees. "It was raining and the red clay roads and the wet grass looked as though a huge cow had been disembowelled and bled over the broad countryside." When they arrive at the station, he tells the farmer, "I feel I need guts and I owed somebody more than money." The farmer, too, is affected by Cow's intensity and by his death. The memory of this "fellow worker, . . . who had come in our midst like a bomb and, bursting himself, planted his fragments in some of us, perhaps, forever" inspires the farmer to return to his home and drive away the foreman who had been cuckolding him.

The narrator boards the train, tries to read Chekhov and cannot. Then, he goes "into the smoker where I sat among mill workers on their way to the mills"[17] thus literally and symbolically joining the workers to begin paying back the "more than money" he owed.

"An Answer for My Uncle" (ca. 1940-1945) portrays a man who is the opposite of Cow, weak, irresponsible, and quick to blame others for his misfortunes. The story, a vignette of Jewish family life, explores what happens when the father's brother and his family come to live in New York with them. The first person narrator is a high school boy. Uncle Meyer has a wife and five children; he works at various semi-skilled jobs, quitting at any slight mistreatment; he looks back to the past, recalling minor triumphs of Jews against their Russian masters. He has a paranoid dislike of gentiles.

Uncle Meyer and his family appear again in Jacob's Son with only minor changes. In fact, some of "An Answer for My Uncle" appears word for word in Jacob's Son, written nearly thirty years later.

Another character who reappears in Field's last novel is the narrator's older brother Jack. In the short story, he taunts Meyer about his fears and his shiftlessness and sneers at his anecdotes of Jewish triumphs. Jack has a pipe "covered with German verses about the soldier who would rather go to his girl than stand guard."[18] In 1971, those German verses are up-dated to "Make love not war" and appear on the pipe of a neighbor, Henry Stein.

In the short story, Meyer and his family go to Israel and fare no better than they had in New York. The "answer" of the title of the story is the narrator's problem. He does not know how to answer the letter from his uncle which is a recital of failure in the Promised Land. In the end of Jacob's Son, Uncle Meyer and some of his children have gone to Israel and are succeeding. Working out the differences between the kind of man Cow was and the kind of man that Uncle Meyer was--in Outside Leaf and, much later, in Jacob's Son--Field was able finally to write that answer for his uncle.

Field's four novels are bildungsroman: stories of adolescent growth. The pattern of growth for the protagonists in these novels is first, the rejection of parents and other authorities; then, the working out of independence; and finally, understanding and acceptance of parents and the past. A short story of adolescence which preceded the novels reveals the depth of suffering such growth can entail.

"Whom the Ox Gored" (1941) tells only of the first phase, rejection of parents and synagogue and their values. The protagonist, Ezekiel, is torn between these old values and the new values of his public high school peers. He ingratiates himself into their company by mocking his religion and by helping these athletes with their schoolwork, even by cheating on tests. When he fails in his visit to a local prostitute, whom all these boys patronize, he cannot bear their taunts. He takes to his bed to avoid the mockery of these boys he has tried so hard to emulate. When his father confronts him with his wickedness and beats him, Ezekiel cuts his own throat with his father's sacrificial knife.

This short narrative is an abortive bildungsroman; the protagonist, being only a boy, has strength enough to reject parents and religion only as long as he can aspire to be accepted by a new group. When they reject him, he cannot return to the stifling routine of school and synagogue nor pursue maturity on his own. He can only withdraw and then destroy himself.

Subsequent to this story, Field showed his heroes persevering in their life-tasks, completing the movement away from family into independence and back to family.

Field's first novel <u>The Outside Leaf</u> (1943), the first of his four bildungsromans, takes place in the tobacco-growing region along the Connecticut River. The subject matter of Realism has always been lower and middle class life; the manner of telling has always included many details of common life. Field is a realistic writer in both matter and manner. He writes of the lower class and he details their homes and farms, jobs and tools. An example of this detail is the four-and-a-half page "Author's Note" at the beginning of <u>The Outside Leaf</u>, which gives an account of how tobacco is grown from planting through curing. Many details of tobacco farming are woven into the story.

Moe Miller, the protagonist of <u>The Outside Leaf</u>, is twenty-six years old, but he is referred to as "the boy" by his parents and by the author, who was then over forty and perhaps thinking of this man as a boy, perhaps suggesting, however, that anyone is a child who has not attained independence.

Moe is taciturn, morose, and irascible, so unlike his parents that he can hardly communicate with them. <u>The Outside Leaf</u> is the story of Moe's year of extremely intense work during which he proves to himself and to the world that he can grow good tobacco and be his own man.

Moe is the first reincarnation of Cow, large, strong, very disciplined, and able to work long hours each day, seven days a week. His self-discipline extends to keeping away from women, unlike Hyman Kahn, the local lady killer who is a foil to Moe. Moe differs from Cow also in his detachment from political and radical thought. An effort to organize the tobacco farmers is treated only incidentally in _The Outside Leaf_. Moe is too busy to study the organization or to help its growth.

Moe rejects his mother and father and even repudiates his nationality. Moe has no respect for his father, because he is not the kind of tough person that Moe wants to become. His father, Israel Miller, is a Russian Jewish immigrant, scholarly, understanding, witty, and wise. He had pursued various trades in order to support his wife and Moe, but his temperament had never been that of a go-getter. He is, in the time covered by the novel, half blind and physically weak. He has given up active work on the farm, and Moe has taken complete charge of it.

Moe has a special dislike for his mother, Esther, because she is over-solicitous for him and somewhat coquettish. She is quite a bit younger than her husband, so he treats her as a girl, but he and Moe also fear that she might attract a younger man and be attracted to him. Moe dislikes Hyman "Genghis" Kahn, because he and Moe's mother seem to have a special affection for one another, and because he lacks self-discipline.

In a dialogue with Anton, an old Polish farm hand, Moe reveals his scorn for the old country. Anton is sad that Hitler had taken Poland. Moe says that Hitler will take Russia, too. Anton wonders how Moe can care so little for the country of his people, saying, "The old country is a mother. America is a wife, a girl. How can you be forgetting the old mother?" Moe replies, "You can forget for once the old hole you come from!"[19]

Later, his father chides him for treating Anton so cruelly, reminding him that Anton is a man, too, and that they all have relatives in the old country.

> "He left a wife and children in Poland. Your mother and I are not stones. Your mother's sister is there; your own blood. After all, you are still a Jew."
>
> "There you go Jewin me again."
>
> Miller was beginning to lose his temper. "I speak to you as a man, then!"[20]

Moe turns away from his father and ends the discussion.

Moe hires Mary Foley, a red-haired girl from a neighboring farm, to help with the farm work. Mary becomes an important element in Moe's maturing, because she is independent and stands up to him. She comes to love him, and she pursues him but always on her own terms. She understands him and wants him to be an autonomous person as much as he does, but she also wants him to be kind, understanding, and compassionate. When he does not fulfill her expectations, she is quick to tell him so or to show her disapproval. Mary is the first of Field's major female characters.

At the end of the novel, Moe has grown a successful crop, proving himself as a farmer, and has married Mary Foley, and he has changed from the alienated, too independent, inarticulate person he was. He has found love and compassion; he understands his mother and father as never before. He is able to express himself and relate to others. Hard work and success have given him assurance; Mary's love and clear vision have given him humanity.

In the end, too, Moe's growth helps his father to greater understanding of himself and his son and to greater courage. He defies his wife and begins to ignore his ailments, promising himself that he will begin to work again.[21] It is he who ponders over the meaning of Moe's chosen occupation and articulates Moe's growth.

Israel Miller relates Moe to the Esau of Genesis, who had been overshadowed by Jacob in life and in the history of the Jews. Jacob had taken Esau's portion of their inheritance and had become the father of the twelve tribes. The scholarly Reb Israel Miller, who had followed the path of Jacob, thinks that now the day of Esau may have come.[22]

Later, after Hyman Kahn is killed, Israel ponders Moe's need for the understanding he had given him and the contrast between Moe and Hyman. He feels that Moe is

> a son for these times--tough as a bull, short-tempered, morose, single-minded as a monk, so utterly unlike her [Israel's wife], unlike himself, so utterly unlike the handsome, hard-riding Absalom of a Hyman, whose death, like a lightning flash had

> revealed to him how close he, too, had come to losing that which gives life its dignity and worth, its immortality.[23]

This novel is dedicated "For My Father, Teacher and Lover of his people," but Reb Israel is not a portrait of Ben Field's own father. This character is based on a farmer in Connecticut whom Field knew and on a family friend who had been on the staff of the _Jewish Farmer_ and had farmed himself after he arrived from Czarist Russia. Field returned to the relationship between a father and a son and the sons of Jacob many years later, and again utilized these two real men as bases for a character.[24]

Piper Tompkins (1946) fulfills the definition of bildungs-roman more completely than the earlier novel, because Piper John Tompkins[25] is an adolescent at the beginning. His growth follows the pattern of rejection, independence, acceptance as he grows to manhood during the course of the novel. Moe Miller had stayed home, pursuing an occupation he already knew well, and fighting his battles with his parents and himself on the spot. Piper leaves home to learn a trade; he is introduced to sex and many kinds of human relationships. He learns responsibility toward himself and others.

In the beginning of the book, Piper is portrayed as unhappy at home except for his hours in the outdoors, hunting, fishing, trapping, and being with his dog. His mentor and model is not his father but Hank Heddy, friend of his grandfather, a bawdy old man who teaches Piper the ways of the woods and gives him an earthy view of life that his parents had not given him.

Piper despises his father for his coldness toward him and his cruelty toward his mother, but he himself does not care for his mother. He feels she is too sweet, too religious, and too manipulative. To keep Piper out of the draft, she manages to get him a job in a defense plant in Hartford, Connecticut.

This scheme of hers eventually works to Piper's advantage, however. When Piper goes to the machine shop, his love for good tools and good workmanship--learned from Hank Heddy--is transferred to the machines, metals, and gauges of his new tasks. Field gives many realistic details of the shop where Piper works and the machining projects that he and others perform. Field had been working as a machinist for four or five years by this time, so the details are accurate.

This novel is proletarian; it deals with the working class and their efforts to better themselves. At first, Piper resists the union people and their leaflets. His foreman suggests to him that the union is for those who cannot think. Piper is so set on independence (the rejection of his parents is part of this mood), that he lets the foreman's suggestion keep him from being open-minded about the union.

Gradually, he sees the unfair, prejudiced tactics and the dishonesty of the foreman and the pusher. He begins to get acquainted with Scotty, the chief maintenance man in the plant, and other union leaders. When he is assigned to assist Scotty, he comes to admire him first as a mechanic, then as a man, and finally as a friend of the workers. He then becomes caught up in the unionization of the machine shop and the entire plant.

The story of the unionization of the plant and the story of Piper's maturation are parallel plots. When Piper is introduced to sex, he dissociates himself from the unionizing work, becoming a girl-chaser and hell-raiser. Not only does he neglect the union work, he becomes less than conscientious about his job, rushing in at the last minute and forcing himself to stay at his machine the required number of hours.

Scotty's daughter Lucy is mentioned fairly early in the book, but it is not until the second half that she becomes a participant in the story and, even later, in the growth of Piper. Their first meetings are at the union organizing sessions that Piper attends at Scotty's home. Lucy seems stuck-up to Piper, not interested in knowing or dating a working man. She prefers college men and even dates Piper's despised foreman once or twice.

As Piper gets to know her, he admires her for her convictions and understands her reluctance to tie herself to a working man. Her father's unionizing activities had caused his family much suffering and the loss of comfort and security. Later, Piper realizes that Lucy likes him very much, but she sometimes acts contrary and puzzles him. Lucy, like Mary Foley in the earlier novel, has standards that she applies to a man. She thus shapes Piper as Mary Foley shaped Moe Miller.

By the end of the book, the plant has been unionized after many struggles and a few broken heads, and Piper has matured. He is a man with a trade and a sense of responsibility for his fellow workers as well as a feeling of obligation to the machines and metals he loves. He has learned about sex, both its irresponsible side and its place in a love relationship. In his new maturity, he can understand some of the reasons for his father's coldness and his mother's manipulative love, and he respects their good qualities as a mature person must.

Piper and Lucy have slept together and have told Scotty of their plan to marry. Before they can marry, however, Piper feels a responsibility to fight in the War. The book ends with Piper on a train going to an Army camp, studying a training manual as he had earnestly studied books on the trade of a machinist and leaflets on unionism, so that he can do as good a job in the Army as he had in the plant.

This last touch of flag-waving Americanism can be attributed to the war atmosphere in which the novel was written more than to Ben Field's attempt to describe America or Americanization. His focus is on personal growth, freedom, responsibility and on workers and their attempts to help themselves. The only places where ethnicity even enters are where the foreman's bias against Jews and Negroes is displayed. These prejudices are rejected by Piper and the other workers. In fact, the foreman's very cruel treatment of a young Negro worker turns many of the other workers toward organization as a means of aiding her and themselves.

The hero of Ben Field's third novel The Last Freshet (1948) is a man in his late forties, so it may not seem accurate to call his story a bildungsroman, but it is a story of maturation, nevertheless. Virgil Doggity, a logger, is a widower whose two sons had been killed in World War II. He must remake his life as a single person, and overcome his grief at the death of his sons; he must also overcome the feeling of futurelessness that a parent must face who outlives his children. He must, as Field has written recently, "make up his mind as to whether he will wither on the stalk or grow new shoots."[26]

The loss of his wife, Emma, is not the trauma that the loss of his sons is. As the story unfolds, the reader learns that Emma had not been the kind of wife that Virgil needed. His nature is feisty, sensual, humorous, optimistic; she had none of these characteristics. He is a mature man, having gone through the rejection phase and achieved independence; he cares nothing for anyone's opinion. He is a good workman, respected by the other loggers. What he has not achieved is interdependence, understanding of himself and others, and the ability to express his feelings fully and freely.

As the story opens, the widows of Virgil's two sons are living with him. Will's widow, Frances, is boisterous and voluptuous, apparently the ideal mate for this son who had inherited the earthy side of Virgil's nature. Ellen, the other daughter-in-law, is pale, serious, and shy. According to Virgil, she is a wet blanket, a wallflower, and a lizard.[27] Frances soon finds herself a man to marry. Ellen stays on with Virge, keeping house for him and aiding neighbors who are ill or in trouble.

Virge is a man's man; he has the admiration of his fellow loggers and respect from the town leaders, even the venal ones who own the town and exploit the workers. He can express anger and speak the bawdy language of workingmen, but he cannot love a woman. His sensual nature had repulsed his wife, and he had turned to prostitutes for satisfaction. The identity crisis caused by the loss of his family provides the occasion for a readiness to change. As Virge gradually learns to relate to Ellen as a person and as a woman, he grows more free and more mature. At the same time, he begins to take on responsibilities in the town and on behalf of his fellow loggers.

Through the relationship with Virge, Ellen, too, is growing. She becomes less repressed, more open and warm, more able to acknowledge and express her feelings. Her repression was caused by being raped as a young girl; her marriage to young Virgil had been --at first--his means of securing aid for his mother in her last illness. Thus, Ellen, though married, had begun to experience real love only just before young Virgil had gone away and been killed.

The turning point in the relationship between Virge and Ellen comes when they decide to marry, because the town gossips think a man and a woman cannot or should not live in the same house with honor. By this time Ellen loves Virge and sees the man he could become, but she realizes the difficulties they have in relating and the psychological bases for those difficulties. Ellen and Virge quarrel over whether to get married in church, as she wishes to, or in a civil ceremony, which would suit the non-religious Virge.

All that night Ellen thinks through her values, rejecting any compromise. She considers Virge's fear of emotion and Emma's lack of response to him. She knows that she must not yield to her own fear of displeasing him, because for the sake of her own maturation she must not give in to fear or repression. In the morning, she tells him she could not live with herself or anyone else if she gave in and had the civil ceremony. He is momentarily angered, until he notices the desire in her face. He loses his grimness and comments on her quiet courage.

What follows is a moment of tenderness which shows Virge's growth in real feeling. His touch shows Ellen her judgment is right and serves to release her feelings, also.

> He stuck out his hand, which she took, and then he did something so strange, warm, and fatherly, as if he saw his boy in her, and at the same time so painful that it seemed to tear her apart. He rumpled her hair before going out. She raised her hands to her face in the characteristic gesture as if to keep her laughter from spilling, her shoulders shook, and when her hands came down they were covered with tears.[28]

One wonders if Virge had ever touched his boys like that. This gesture is, then, a release of tenderness to a young girl--who in a sense is like a child to Virge--which, at the same time, is a gesture of love to a woman. Ellen's reaction suggests that she realizes all the meanings of that gesture, and through it, she, too, grows because this tender "warm, and fatherly" touch counteracts the brutal handling she had received from the older man who had raped her.

Ben Field demonstrates here both knowledge of people and their psychological growth and great skill in saying much in few words.

Ellen consults the rascally old town doctor for release from her fears of sex. In the scene in Dr. Ormsby's office, Field has the doctor express his values. The doctor's message to Ellen is that sex is natural and good, but it should not be paramount, and that each person should have a job to do in the world and do it wholeheartedly.[29]

At the end of the book, Virge and Ellen are married. Both of them are more free and more adult than they have ever been, full of love for each other and the joy of life. Virge has become the whole man that lack of love had prevented him from becoming. His humor and optimism can now be exuberantly expressed in work and in loving.

In addition to Virge and Ellen's relationship, <u>The Last Freshet</u> explores other man-woman relationships. An older couple--age-peers of Virge--also figure in the story. The man is sensuous but taciturn; the woman hides her sensuousness in prudery. She is like Virge's Emma; the man is persevering and one-track-minded enough to finally break through the prudery.

The burly, boorish old doctor appears in several scenes in the book. His solid values and crude habits are given in some detail. He lives with a mistress, who is seen only as a beautiful figure at a distance among her flowers and heard only as the sound of beautiful laughter. The suggestion is that this gracious, now aging, woman assuages the doctor's pain at the stupidity, cruelty, and hypocrisy that he sees around him.

Ray Wilson and his wife are foils to Virge and Ellen. Ray is an ex-state trooper, a fascist at heart. He considers his emotions to be weaknesses, so he represses them, becoming more ugly and cruel and less human. He is not free to love his dumpy wife and fulfills her healthy sexual demands only when he must. His wife is a teacher, but she is not intelligent enough to analyze her husband's problems nor compassionate enough to solve them, as Ellen solved Virge's. The relationship between these two people can only hurt them as the years go by, in contrast to the relationship of Ellen and Virge, which makes each of them more complete.

Ray feels inferior physically and fears the responsibilities that come with parenthood. He fears his father-in-law, who is the owner of the logging company, and he fears the loggers when he is made foreman over them. This fearful man with his fascist tendencies is Field's foreshadowing of the attitudes of many "little people" during the Red Scare of the fifties. He plans to attend a conference of law enforcement officials and American Legion members, which is being called to discuss "equipment and methods with which to recognize the enemies of law and order of whatever stripe in the smallest of communities."[30]

His point of view on law and order is contrasted with the doctor's when Ray goes to the doctor's messy office for a check-up. In discussing the loggers' fight for better working conditions, the doctor tells Ray that a scientist had experimented with water fleas. He had starved them "and found they live longer on hunger. Give them water, hunger, and keep them in their place."[31] Ray is shocked at the doctor's understanding of him and at this rephrasing of his point of view.

> Ray was no fool; he sensed that behind all the filth and seeming disorder there was a freedom, a law and order, a strength which made him feel like a child and helped explain how this man had broken with his own kind and forsaken a brilliant career as a surgeon to become a doctor among hillbillies and country jakes.[32]

The loggers' fight with their boss is a parallel plot to the bildungsroman, but the fight is less complicated than Piper Tompkins' and the machinists' struggle against the large factory. By the end of the novel, Virge and the loggers have won some concessions from their boss, and Virge has been made foreman, thus insuring better treatment for the men, and demonstrating that he is now ready for responsibility in a way that he had not been before.

Ben Field's latest novel <u>Jacob's Son</u> (1971) is long and detailed; it reworks some of Field's themes, events, and characters of the 1940's.[33] It is a bildungsroman as were his earlier proletarian novels, portraying members of the lower middle class in a realistic manner. The major difference between the new work and the three earlier ones is that Jacob's Son deals explicitly with the religious traditions of the Jewish characters and with the problem of Americanization.

In this novel, the protagonist, Michael Berkowitz, grows from an eighteen-year-old just out of high school to a very manly twenty-two year old. The narrative is set in a working class Jewish neighborhood in Brooklyn and on a farm in upstate New York. Michael lives with his mother and with the memory of his father, who had died when Michael was twelve, soon after the boy's Bar Mitzvah. When the story opens, Michael is beginning his rebellion against the shadow of his father, Jacob, a noted scholar, who is still revered by the members of the Tree of Life synagogue and by his gentile neighbors as well.

Jacob's widow, Rebecca, is only forty at the beginning of the novel; the fact that she was much younger than her husband is important in their relationship.

Michael is a brilliant student, trained by his father. He has a great love of nature, learned from his father's example. He has inherited his father's weakness, a chest condition such that any exertion brings on nausea, pain, and faintness. This condition may be psychosomatic. In any case, it serves as a symbol. The more Michael rids himself of the shade of his father and expectations that he will emulate his father's career, the less he suffers this weakness.

Michael's mother and the leaders of the Jewish community expect him to attend college and become a scholar and teacher as his father had been. He is tired of books and learning; he wants to become a farm hand. He wants to evolve his own values, to become an independent thinker, and to be a disciplined and responsible person. The novel details Michael's efforts to move away from the traditional roles assigned him while still carrying the weight of family responsibility.

The rejection, independence, acceptance pattern is followed in this novel. Michael rejects the memory of his father and his father's profession. He rejects his mother for her coquettish, sentimental, flighty, over-solicitous ways. He rejects his religion, his childhood friends, any and every form of dependence and group membership.

In rejecting his religion, he also rejects a Jewish dislike of gentiles and a willingness to shirk responsibility, which he sees as one possible Jewish reaction under stress. His insights about the importance of responsibility are reinforced by the work of the Russian Jewish poet Chaim Nachman Bialik, who narrated the story of Russian Jewish men who hid behind barrels and watched as their wives and children were violated. Michael abhors this trait in his people and consciously strives to become forceful, responsible, and courageous. He analyzes his own behavior in Bialik's terms, noting when moral weakness makes him hide behind a barrel and when he learns to stand manfully and fight.

Michael rejects his ties to his people and their traditions both emotionally and intellectually. He speaks of his rejections when he feels he will be understood, but most often he remains silent or becomes surly, because he cannot make himself understood and because he cannot carry out these rejections by actually leaving his family. Even though his mother works, he feels he must bear some responsibility for her until she remarries.

Jacob's Son is dedicated "for the men and women who met in my father's house, the house with the privet hedges." Part I of the book is called "The House with the Privet Hedges: 1930." There is ambiguity here, because there are two characters who live in houses with privet hedges: Joshua Birnbaum, a baker, and Hershel Bendel, a medical doctor, who is also superintendent of the Talmud school. Dr. Bendel is the character based on Field's father, according to Field, and Birnbaum is a composite figure.[34] Dr. Bendel's garden is described as having roses and hydrangeas as the father's garden had in "An Answer for My Uncle." Dr. Bendel is witty, forceful, shrewd, and rather gross in speech and manner. Michael rebels against Bendel's attempts to mold him into an image of his father, but it is not primarily Bendel that Michael must struggle to reject. It is Jacob, his father, gentle, ingratiating, the pillar of the community, the inheritor and transmitter of a religious and cultural heritage, that he must overcome.

Jacob Berkowitz is a more commanding figure than Israel Miller of Outside Leaf, but there are resemblances between these two men. They are both scholars, both physically weak, both--as Field has recently written--"gentle, compassionate men with a great deal of tolerance for those whose religion differs from theirs."[35] They are both married to a woman much younger than they and much more eager for physical love.

It is possible that Jacob Berkowitz symbolizes more than the parent; he may also symbolize the weak-bodied scholar that Michael does not want to become. Further, because his name is Jacob, and Field makes reference to the Jews as "Jacob's sons," Jacob Berkowitz may also symbolize the Jewish cultural and religious heritage, and even the heritage of foreignness, which Michael rejects.

Part I of the novel is mainly exposition--introduction of the characters and of Michael's aspirations and the factors which prevent him from fulfilling them. The first action in Michael's rebellion comes in this section when he leaves Brooklyn to work as a farmhand on Reuben Gross's farm in the summer of 1930. The name of Reuben's farm, "Green Fields," is an allusion to a drama by Peretz Hirschbein. The film version was summarized in New Masses as "the story of a Talmudic student in czarist Russia who leaves the temple and goes out into the world to search for Truth and to learn the ways of real people."[36] This summary is almost a statement of Michael Berkowitz's quest. Reuben had been a friend of Jacob Berkowitz; he is a large, strong man, who has a red-haired mistress, Kathy O'Brien. He is like Cow and Moe Miller in size and strength but not in self-discipline. Michael admires Reuben's skill as a farmer, his wisdom and Tolstoyan gentleness, but Michael clearly sees Reuben's lack of discipline and moral courage. He gladly apprentices himself to Reuben to learn farming, but he feels Reuben's weaknesses are the opposite of what he wishes to become.

Part II of the novel is called "Uncle Meyer: 1932" and it is here that some parts of Field's short story of the early forties is repeated. Uncle Meyer again descends on his brother's family with his anecdotes, his pie-in-the-sky notions, and his paranoia about gentiles. Field has made a few changes in Meyer's family, however. In "An Answer for My Uncle" he has a son, Judah, who has a harelip and seems to be mentally retarded, twin daughters Bessie and Tessie, a baby, and then, later, another baby Isaiah, born in a caul. In the novel, his children are Eva, Gertrude, Isaiah, who has a harelip and the same mannerisms as the earlier Judah, Bessie, and later, Jacob, who is born in a caul.

Michael finds nothing to admire in his uncle; he epitomizes the very Jew that Bialik wrote against. Michael and his mother take on the burden of Meyer and his family, obtaining for them the job of live-in caretakers for the Bendels. Michael and Rebecca suffer with Meyer through his hirings and firings from various jobs, trying in every way to support Meyer and his family.

Michael is caught in this family responsibility and in family expectations. He does not want to attend college or become a teacher, but he fulfills the expectation and goes to college, earning his way by teaching part-time in the Talmud school. He studies very hard and obtains his degree in three years, feeling then that he has discharged these two obligations.

He still must wait for his freedom until Uncle Meyer is financially secure. First, Michael organizes a house painting business with himself, Meyer, and Henry Stein as working partners. The three of them build up a trade in Brooklyn, but when Henry and Michael leave the business, Meyer cannot carry on alone. Meyer and his family try farm life with Reuben and Michael, but only Isaiah takes to it.

Meyer is neither competent nor realistic. He always feels that the goyim are harassing him and clings to his dream of living in the Holy Land, where he is sure he will achieve success.

Parts II and III of the novel are very complex, not because of a subplot of organizational work as in two of Field's earlier novels, but because of the interplay between Michael's maturation and his part in helping each member of his extended family find a place in the world and a measure of autonomy. Field is displaying in this fictional way a dream that Michael Novak has also set forth. In a section of The Rise of the Unmeltable Ethnics called "The Dream of New Work," he says that "work should be imagined as part of the tissue, network, and organism of family and growth."[37] Michael, the former Talmudic student in search of real people, observes the other characters' needs and strengths. He uses Bialik's warning against hiding, against moral weakness, as a touchstone for behavior. He rejects his uncle's fanatical clannishness and his prejudice against the goyim. The complexity of the novel is compounded by the presence of many families--the Bendels, the Birnbaums, the Steins, and others--and their relationships with Michael, his mother, Meyer's family, and the memory of Jacob.

Michael rejects his own peers in his quest for autonomy, because they are caught up in a radical movement. He has a particular dislike for one of them, Sidney "El Cid" Kahn. As the story progresses, Michael's dislike is revealed as a child's intuitive response to the clandestine relationship between his mother and El Cid. Rebecca had been almost forced by Jacob to take his favorite pupil as a lover. Rebecca had loved El Cid and still has a special affection for him, tainted with guilt.

The sexual relationship between the young wife of the elderly scholar and a brash young man is made explicit in this novel. Such a relationship (between Rachel and "Genghis" Kahn) was only hinted at in <u>The Outside Leaf</u>.

The only two young persons that Michael admires are his cousin Eva and Henry "The Fish" Stein. Henry is a vulgar, bawdy girl-chaser, half Jewish and half Catholic by heritage, totally iconoclastic by inclination. He taunts Michael for his sexual repression and angers him with vulgar innuendos. Michael despises the Fish for his lack of discipline, especially in sexual matters, but he can only admire the Fish's independence and defiance of God and man.

Eva, the eldest of Meyer's children, is tough-minded and independent. She works to pay her way through college so that she can become a teacher even though she must work for gentiles in defiance of her father. She defies him also when she questions his treatment of the younger children. Eva loves Michael and lets him know it on occasion, but she does not pursue him.

Michael is disappointed by Reuben's lack of defiance. Reuben's resolve to marry his red-haired Irish mistress collapses when the Jewish elders in the nearby village gossip about the two of them. He then severs his relationship with Kathy and renews his courtship of Rebecca, begun many years before in Russia. Both Reuben and Rebecca had been married to persons much older than themselves. To marry someone of the same age and the same sensual nature now would seem a kind of closure or fulfillment.

Before they can marry, Reuben is killed. Michael feels that the accident is an indirect result of Reuben's moral weakness in toadying to the Jews who had whispered about him and Kathy. Michael is grateful for all that Reuben had taught him about farming, but now Michael has outstripped him both as a farmer and as a man of principle.

Rebecca is injured in the same accident. As she recovers, Michael realizes that she will always be flighty and coquettish; it is her nature to be so, but he also sees the strong woman under all the nonsense and forced happiness. He now knows that she had always understood him and had often been deliberately playful, thus demonstrating to him that humor and light-heartedness are necessary to life. At the end, Michael knows that it is Rebecca who is the strong member of the party as she and Meyer, his wife, and Isaiah, Bessie, and Jacob emigrate to Israel.

Michael has helped Rebecca realize her strength; he has helped Eva when she needed him. He has taken the child Isaiah--fearful, withdrawn, and almost inarticulate--and raised him to be a good farmhand, capable, happy, and able to express himself. The only one he could not help was the sensuous, headstrong Gertrude. She had loved him and offered herself to him. When he refused her, she went to Henry Stein. She had had a baby by Henry, but neither of them was responsible enough for the commitment of marriage. Michael feels some guilt about Gertrude and hopes that Henry will return from Spain and marry her.

These two failures aside, Michael has succeeded at all the tasks set him: he had finished college and had been a successful teacher to please those who would put him in that mold; he has succeeded in helping Uncle Meyer and his younger children to start a new life in the Promised Land. More important, he has made himself into the man he wanted to become--self-reliant, disciplined, principled.

In a final confrontation with Dr. Bendel and some of the other elders of the Tree of Life[38] synagogue, one of the men questions Michael about following the thought of the poet Bialik but not following him to Israel. Michael replies, "I follow footsteps which lead in the direction I am going. If they don't, I walk alone."[39] Michael has chosen America as his country. He knows he has succeeded in his aspirations to choose his own loyalties when he wins a verbal joust with Dr. Bendel by saying:

> "Papa was concerned with building a new life out of American materials. He loved America for all it had done for him. I am building my life out of American materials in a different way. I have naturalized myself here. I have taken out my own papers. I have worked on a farm and in the woods. Palestine is holy because Jews built their lives there. The land where a man labors, builds his house, his life, that land is holy. I have built my house, my life here. O'Brien's woods is my homeland, and the brook there is my River Jordan!"[40]

Michael appears to reject the faith of his father. In explaining the allusive meaning of Tree of Life, however, Field explains Michael's attitude toward the synagogue.

> Now to Michael, the synagogue is not representative of the whole Tree of Life. . . . What he is after is a many-branched life, consisting, first, of labor, the life of the hands. That may help to explain the importance of the synagogue in his life. He is not in complete rebellion against it. Surely, not in rebellion against the prophets whom he loved and whose ethical teachings had a profound influence on him and are parts of the services daily and during the High Holydays.[41]

As a critic who has read only the first third of the trilogy, I must suspect that Field is anticipating a change in Michael's attitude which will take place later than this first novel. Michael does not attend Holyday services nor quote the prophets in Jacob's Son. He has reconciled himself to parents and some authorities in this book but not to the religion as such. Michael then tells Dr. Bendel and the others his plan to leave the farm and become a logger. Here is the statement of the man of independence, the man who has searched for Truth: "To work with my hands is direct, simple, honest, and free. No one gets between me and my hands when I put an axe to a tree. No one gets between me and the field when I sow rye."[42]

After this confrontation, Michael takes Eva home. He begins to realize the strength in her; her independence and good sense impress him. He is able to express his philosophy to her. The reader feels that these two young people have made their identities and are now ready for a conscious interdependence, based not on tradition or family expectations, but on mutual caring.

The theme of personal growth and maturation is constant in Field's work; Jacob's Son is different, however, not only in the explicit description of the ethnic group, but in the totally independent, single-handed growth of his latest protagonist. There is no workers' organization; there is no sexy, tough-minded girl to tease Michael into compassion and interdependence. Likewise, religious and cultural heritages are repudiated as models except for the work of Bialik and only when Bialik repudiates qualities in Jews that Michael himself despises and speaks as a man calling to everyman.[43]

In Field's short stories and reportage and in two early novels, Piper Tompkins and The Last Freshet, he was pro-union and pro-Marx. His characters believed in concerted action, either union organizations or loose groupings of friends who worked against a particular boss. For example, "In the Grass" (1932) is the story of two farm laborers who beat up their boss for hiding in a thicket observing their work. He had exploited and humiliated them; this ambush is their only recourse to alleviate the frustration of the powerless.

In *Jacob's Son* Field is anti-Marxist and anti-farmers' union. Some of Michael's peers sympathize with the Marxists, especially a Jewish shoemaker who moves from their neighborhood to Mexico and other places, trying to organize workers. Some of them, including Henry the Fish Stein, go to Spain to fight with the Loyalists. Michael dissociates himself from these friends for fear of getting caught up with them in these movements.

Eugene Kahn travels to Russia and writes articles about collective farms. When he visits Reuben's farm, he tries to persuade Reuben and Michael to join a farmers' union. Reuben replies that only farmers who cannot make a success of farming want a union. When Eugene suggests that Reuben go as a delegate to a farmers' convention, he refuses and relays the invitation to Michael, who curtly answers "Not interested."[44] Michael's opinion of Eugene is that he is a "great literary shakes" who knows nothing about farming, "had never handled a pitchfork or a plow, yet he was giving advice as if having tasted Karl Marx's matzos in the Soviet Union, he had become an expert on farming."[45]

In the three early novels, the protagonist grows more mature as he grows more competent in his work. His independence is achieved through this growing competence and through rejection of family. But late in the story, it is the goading behavior of a girl which forces each man to face himself and his values in a new way. Each girl is seen as sexually attractive, honest, fearless, humorous, and puzzlingly inconsistent.

When Moe or Piper or Virge were puzzled or irritated by the behavior of a girl, they learned to see their own behavior from the girl's point of view. What intrigues the reader, as well as Field's protagonists, is that the women are not inconsistent; their behavior is consistent with their values. It is the men who are inconsistent, who lack some aspect of character necessary to a full human personality. The men in the early novels thus become more compassionate, more understanding, more rounded as persons because of their relationships with these women of integrity.

In Field's latest novel, the good, strong-minded Eva observes Michael, but they do not interact in the way that the earlier couples did. Eva tells Michael that he reminds her of Ibsen's Dr. Stockman who said that "that man is strongest who stands alone,"[46] and then reminds him that she needed his help one time. At the end of the book, Michael articulates his philosophy of independence to her.

> "A man is like a fish, living off his yolk sac until he matures and becomes his own creature. If he becomes dependent on the Sarahs and the Terachs of the world, they become his yolk sac and he goes under."[47]

Michael drives away from his hour with Eva, feeling free and competent, eager to begin his new logging job. But the hour with Eva marks a new phase of their relationship. He grew to be his own creature without much help from her or anyone. Now, if they create a relationship, neither of them will go under.

Conclusion

Throughout his life Ben Field has been concerned with identity, personal growth and freedom, self-discipline and responsibility for one's self. In his early stories he contrasted the strong, responsible, rebellious man with the weak, dependent man. Cow is the most notable of the strong men, but there are also Pop in "In the Grass," Lou Benson who appears in three short stories in The Cock's Funeral, and others. Uncle Meyer is the opposite: he is weak, unable and unwilling to take the responsibility for his own support or his own failures.

The wish to depart from a scholarly tradition and become a worker is thematic in Field's work. I queried him as to whether this theme was linked to his early Marxist sympathies or whether it was more personal. He replied:

> It is more personal. Marxism had something to do with it, but it stems from a reaction against my early life as in Michael's case. I envied the rebel because I as a youngster was an obedient one, the "good boy," the least venturesome of the boys on the block.
>
> "Cow," Moe Miller, Piper Tompkins, Michael Berkowitz, each one of these was a No-sayer. "Cow" a rebel against our capitalist society. Moe against his father's scholarly way of life, his ineffectiveness as a farmer, his being a man of the book. Piper Tompkins has no use for books. There was a time in the 1930's when I too

> dreamed of dropping writing, forgetting about books, and becoming a farmer and a farm organizer. I admired the strong man, one with physical courage. Obviously during that period Marxism strengthened my reaction against the old life of the classroom and the type-writer. Me for the fields and woods and the machine shop![48]

The value of Field's work can be assessed both as to matter and manner. The Outside Leaf is a good beginning; Piper Tompkins is a good story, but somewhat time-bound. The Last Freshet, the story of a mature man, is valuable as an indication that growth need never stop; that life holds rewards for those who reach inward for new resources and outward for new relationships and new adventures. All of these novels are written in Field's forceful style; all of them have humor and movement. The Last Freshet has a special quality of rising life, as a stream rises when the snow melts.

Field's early work shows a whiplash energy; his words and sentences work and pound. Jacob's Son is slower-moving, more allusive, but much of that energy lives below the surface. The descriptions of work in field and barn are no less detailed than in the earlier stories.

Jacob's Son is valuable as an exposition of the traditions of Jewish life: the life of the scholar-sage, Jacob, which many other Jewish writers have also described, and the life of the workman, Esau, which Field has lived. It is valuable as a chronicle of Jewish family life: the conditional love of the father, modeling and enforcing the orthodox life; the love of the mother and her motivation in loving unconditionally, excessively. It also depicts religious customs and their changing significance, and it explores several attitudes toward gentiles.

Field dealt with family relationships in many of his stories and all of his early novels, mostly in the pattern of rejection, independence, acceptance. When he returned to such relationships in Jacob's Son, he made his hero take on the burden of family and struggle to transfer to each member the burden of responsibility for himself. Field seems to be saying that it is not enough to reject a family; independence cannot be gained if there are dependent souls all around one.

Field indicated a repudiation of his own Russian Jewish people in The Outside Leaf when Moe Miller easily dismisses reminders of his heritage as "Jewin me." Moe's dismissal was too hasty; Ben Field had to repeat it many years later.

Another interpretation of Field's final book is also possible. Michael's very curt refusal of Eugene's invitation to join the farmers' union is indicative of Field's changed attitude toward group membership and revolutionary activity. Another indication is his treatment of the Marxist shoemaker. Freund is prominent in the first scene of Jacob's Son; thereafter his whereabouts and activities are followed by Michael's friends, but Michael avoids him and those friends because they are getting caught up in an ideology.

By the time Field was ready to write this novel, to repudiate Marxism was outmoded, either because many early radicals had already repudiated it or because the Red Scare no longer scares people. The character Freund looms very large in the first episode of the book, but he becomes a shadowy figure who does not influence the protagonist or add to the narrative. Field is dismissing Marxism and ideological commitment in the person of this shadowy figure.

Field's comment on the revolutionary quality of his work is:

> I did at one time consider my writing revolutionary. I would call "Cow" and a number of other stories in THE COCK'S FUNERAL revolutionary. "Jacob's Son" is not revolutionary in the same sense, that is, explicitly politically of the Left. It does not raise the Red Flag. On the contrary, it seems to lower it. But "Jacob's Son" is definitely progressive in the broadest sense of the word, which some of my friends who reviewed it for the Communist press were unable to see. I no longer believe that writing in the United States at the present time can be a revolutionary activity, in the narrow sense of the phrase, and be effective, and a reflection of the American scene.[49]

In one answer to a question from me, Field refers to "social realism or socialist realism" as "a lot of balderdash."[50] In a subsequent letter, he clarifies that statement.

> My use of "balderdash" was a sign of the feeling of outrage which has been with me for years because of the two terms, social realism and socialist realism, by the Stalins, the Shdanovs, the Faithful in this country to bulldoze writers into presenting a one-sided view of reality, to turn out boiler-plate characters, to write as if life were an erector set.[51]

Field mentions that Chekhov was his favorite short story writer as a young man but that during his proletarian period, he had dropped Chekhov. In clarifying his position on socialist realism, he utilizes a metaphor from Chekhov, who is again his favorite.

> Now if the central canon of socialist realism is, according to the 1934 Congress of Soviet Writers "the truthful, historically concrete representation of reality in its revolutionary development," I've got myself out on a bough which is not in flowering and [am] sawing away at it. For I do believe in the essence of what the Congress was stating. Chekhov put it simply, differently when he said the writer should show men not only as they are but as they may be. In other words, the writer like the hunter with the raised gun aims it ahead of the bird in flight in order to bring down the bird. Aiming at the bird will not get the bird down, not the bird Man. For man is in action, man changes in a Heracletan [sic] world.[52]

Membership in a family and membership in an ethnic group are the two "yolk sacs" Field has Michael remove from himself, even though his maturation is heavily weighted with responsibility. He must stive to make others as mature and as responsible for themselves as he is. <u>Jacob's Son</u> is a narrative, not of one son only, but of many sons and daughters of the Biblical Jacob; some who grow, and a few who fail to grow.

Reuben, physically powerful, and Meyer, physically weak, do not grow. Reuben is killed, and Meyer is provided with Israel for a yolk sac and Rebecca to cajole him into doing for himself.

Henry Stein is fiercely independent of authority but a slave to his sexual needs. Gertrude has always defied authority, but she, like Henry, could not control her passions. At the end of the novel, there is hope that Gertrude is changing; by accepting the responsibility for her child, she is accepting self-discipline, also.

Michael, Eva, Rebecca, and Isaiah have taken responsibility for themselves. They are competent in their chosen occupations; they are able to support themselves both financially and emotionally.

The conclusion that can be posited from this analysis of Field's life and work is that he is a second generation immigrant who hung suspended between identity as an American and another identity. He worked all his life to express maturation; he aimed to tell of progress and human growth. But in working for a progressive movement, his maturation was caught up in group membership. In his early writing, he dismissed family, ethnic group, and religious heritage, but he was not thereby independent of group membership. He found his identity in a movement--Marxism and the organization of working men--just as some young people in the seventies are finding their identities in campus action movements or communes. To reject the heritage of one's blood and then turn for identity to a group united by work ideology or a cause is to substitute one group identity for another.

Field's protagonists illustrate his working life as a teacher, farmer, machinist, and logger. Michael gave up teaching at twenty-two; Field not until he was nearly forty. In 1943, Field wrote of a Jewish scholar-father speaking of the possibility of Esau's day being at hand, but he did not convince himself. In 1948 he wrote of Dr. Ormsby who rejected his father's religion, his politics, and his expectations to go and work among "country jakes." But it was not until Field's late years that he could write of the scholar-father as dead and express his freedom from the yolk sacs of heritage and ideological group.

For Field himself, it seems to me, Jacob's Son is a break-through and a summing-up. He has found his identity as Esau's son, as an American worker, through this return to his identity as part of the group he had rejected. He is able to dismiss easily his long affiliation with an ideological group, but in an almost Faulknerian way, he can describe his independence only against a background of family and congregation and ethnic group. He says a man is a fish who must beware of yolk sacs. He seems to have moved in his life from the yolk sac of family to the yolk sac of labor movement. Finally, in Jacob's Son, he depicts the mature fish, one who is not in a yolk sac of ideology, but in the mingled waters of ethnic heritage and American life.

CHAPTER VI

THOMAS BELL--THE CHOICE OF THE BEST IN AMERICA

Biography

Thomas Bell was a sensitive, thoughtful man, loving, creative, realistic, and hopeful. The characters he created reflect his sensitivity, his ability to love, and his realistic appraisal of what was wrong with American society and the burdensome, restricted lives many Americans endured. Even when his own life became a burden in his last illness, Bell continued to learn, to seek new experiences and to shape them creatively, and to develop himself.

Bell tried many kinds of crafts as well as the craft of writing, and when the choice had to be made, he chose writing. He served an apprenticeship as a romantic writer and then chose the mode of realism. At the height of his powers as a writer, he wrote of his Slovak heritage and American values. He reiterated those values in a partial autobiography at the very end of his life.

Philip Rahv has written that "the principle of realism requires . . . above all a give-and-take relation between the ego and experience."[1] In charting Bell's life and then analyzing his writings, this give and take become clear. Analysis and discussion of Bell's work is greatly aided by the partial autobiography, _In the Midst of Life_; other printed biographical sources are meagre.[2] His own suffering and death and his changing attitudes toward them interested him and troubled him in the months he wrote In the Midst of Life, but he wrote also about other interests; his past, his thoughts on authorship, on America, and its possible future. Some of these interests will be mentioned in this introductory biography section; others will be discussed where pertinent to the discussion of his books.

Thomas Belejcak was born on March 7, 1903 in Braddock, Pennsylvania, a small town near Pittsburgh, the son of an immigrant steel worker and bartender. He was the oldest of four children. His father died of a contagious disease when Thomas was eleven. The family was Catholic and although Bell repudiated religion in his early twenties,[3] he reminisces in his late years about his mother's attitude toward bread. She made a sign of the cross over a fresh loaf before cutting it, and she trained her children to kiss any piece that fell to the floor.[4]

In contemplating his imminent death from cancer at fifty-seven, Bell thought about his father, who had died at thirty-nine, on Thomas' own birthday.

> I imagine that my father must have glanced at me more than once while I was growing up and envied me briefly, envied me not only my youth but my having been born in America, my speaking better English at six than he could speak at thirty-five, my casual acceptance of comforts and luxuries (gas lights, meat on the table every day except Friday, running water--cold--in the kitchen, oilcloth on the parlor floor and an outhouse to which only we had the key) such as in his own childhood he had not even dreamed existed.[5]

A steel mill town is not the place to give a person a love of nature, but Bell had at least one moment, at fourteen, when he was tuned in to the earth and sky.

> City-bred, I have had little firsthand contact with the natural world. . . . Yet now and then, . . . [when] I do come within touching distance of something unfamiliar, as before the sea at night, . . . I experience feelings I can neither name nor altogether enjoy. Surprisingly, they bring back memories of a half-forgotten spring night when I, a boy of fourteen, went to the outdoor privy up the hillside from our ramshackle house in Munhall Hollow, and stripped off my shirt and trousers and then slid cautiously around to the back of the privy, . . . and stood there . . . looking up at the hill and the stars, quivering with emotions that seemed to be coming at me from the earth and sky like invisible rays, . . . letting the whirling, pulsating universe permeate my skinny body. After a while I crept back into the privy and dressed and returned to the house. My mother was probably doing the supper dishes, my sisters and brother at their homework around the oil lamp on the table, my grandfather smoking his pipe by the cooling stove--all unaware that a young pagan had just returned from participating in an ancient mystery.[6]

Thomas began to work at fourteen or fifteen as a helper in a glass company in Glassport, Pennsylvania. At sixteen, he worked as an apprentice electrician in a steel mill in Donora, Pennsylvania. It was during his sixteenth year that his mother died of tuberculosis in a sanitarium. Two years later, he was working on the furnaces in a steel mill in Braddock and writing a column for the Braddock _News-Herald_, using first his initials as a by-line and then the pseudonym Thomas Bell.[7]

His formal education may have ended at that time, but he read "so voraciously that I was little more than an appetite let loose in a library,"[8] and he wrote from the time he was very young.[9]

His self-education is manifested in In the Midst of Life by allusions to or quotations from Montaigne, Seneca, Keats, Bertrand Russell, Dumas, Proust, Thoreau, Ambrose Bierce (who also wrote a book called In the Midst of Life), Aldous Huxley, James Joyce, and James Branch Cabell, whose novel Jurgen influenced Bell's first novel. He also taught himself to love classical music, mentioning in the course of his musings the names of Bach, Beethoven, Mozart, and Bruckner and their works. He did not have a metaphysical turn of mind; he quickly found the work of Kierkegaard, Heidegger, Kafka, Camus, Sartre, Meister Eckhart, and other philosophers not fruitful for him.[10]

In 1922, Bell went to New York where he worked as a mechanic in a Long Island Rail Road shop. He shipped out twice as a seaman on a freighter, working in a shelving place between these journeys.[11] Later, he worked as buyer, cataloguer, and salesman in Schulte's Book Store in New York City. Bell was able to draw upon all these work experiences later, portraying them very authentically in the lives of his characters.

Bell's first novel The Breed of Basil was published in 1930, dedicated to his sisters and brother, Pauline, Evelyn, and Anthony.[12] The following year, he wrote an introduction for an edition of Boccaccio's Questions of Love which was published in a limited edition.

He married Marie Benedetti, herself the daughter of an immigrant mother, in St. Rosalie's Church in Brooklyn on January 2;

1932. He had a bout of pneumonia and was very ill during the first year of his marriage. He was ordered by his doctor to make a choice: he could work or he could write, but he could not do both. With his wife's consent, he decided to devote his time to writing.[13] Marie worked at Norcross, and they lived on her earnings. His second novel The Second Prince is dedicated to her. In this book, the heroine is of Italian descent, but in his later novels, the heroines--although based on Marie--have the same kind of vaguely Anglo-Saxon names as the heroes. In 1936 the story of their first two years of married life appeared as All Brides Are Beautiful, which was made into a film From This Day Forward in 1948.[14] Bell and his wife spent almost a year in Hollywood in 1936-37 while Thomas was under contract to MGM.

Bell became ill in 1940, and after an exploratory operation, was placed on a strict diet. He read the galley proofs of his third novel while in the hospital.[15] This novel, a story of his family and his Slovak people, was published under the title Out of This Furnace in 1941 and dedicated "To the Memory of my mother, my father, and my grandfather." This book is structured in four parts: focussing first on an immigrant from Slovakia, then on his son-in-law, on his daughter, and finally, on his grandson.

Bell was again hospitalized in 1942 and "came damned close" to dying at the age of thirty-nine as his father had.[16]

When his fourth novel Till I Come Back to You was published in 1943, Bell was featured on the cover of the Saturday Review of

June 26. A play The World's Full of Girls was based on this novel, but it was badly adapted and thus ran only nine performances on Broadway in December of that year. It was badly received by the critics[17] and by Bell himself.[18]

Bell began to publish short stories about this time, usually in women's magazines. Some of these were reprinted in London, also in women's magazines. These are slight fictions about young people meeting and falling in love or being in love though married. The only notable feature, for the present purpose, is the exact detail of machinist's work and other mechanical tasks, which apparently stem from Bell's own work experiences. The most important of his short stories "The Man Who Made Good in America" about Slovak workers was printed in Mainstream in 1947 and reprinted in an anthology Our Lives, American Labor Stories in 1948.

The last of Bell's novels was There Comes a Time (1946), the story of a man who had come from Pennsylvania and who took part in the unionization of the bank where he worked.

Bell suffered a writing bloc about this time, producing only one or two short stories a year. He sought the help of an analyst to overcome his anxiety neurosis. He later writes of this period:

> Marie kept me comparatively normal and human when I was in a fair way to becoming so inhibited, so imprisoned in my own mind and body that even analysis couldn't have helped me. Marie saved me in time; my problems and conflicts didn't become really troublesome until I was almost fifty, and analysis was able to help me even at that psychologically advanced age.[19]

In 1955 Bell and his wife moved to Santa Cruz, California, where his brother Tony lives, and opened a small stationery, gift, and office supply store. They were content to be shopkeepers, Bell noting in his autobiography his view that a storekeeper must be "a generous soul who likes to give pleasure to people."[20] His wife comments that in his writing Thomas "gave much of himself."[21] Thus, although his writing career was almost over, Bell was still engaged in giving of himself to please others. Thomas and Marie staggered their hours in the store, so that he would not have to rush off to work early in the morning, which he was not used to doing, and so that he would have some time to be alone. He liked the store and waiting on and observing customers, but he liked, he writes "as I always have, privacy and solitude, they are as necessary to me as air."[22]

Bell was informed in September 1958 that he had a sarcoma, a malignant tumor attached to his liver and pancreas, and that he had only a few more months to live. On February 23, 1959, he began to write his thoughts and feelings about imminent death, because, as he writes, he would have liked to read a book such as the one he was writing:

> a book in which the author . . . had written about the things that interested and troubled him, in a way that would interest--and instruct and I hoped strengthen--me.[23]

As long as he was able, he continued to help his wife in the store and do some of the housework, as he had done in the first years of their marriage. The last chapter of In the Midst of Life was written in October 1960. Bell died on January 17, 1961, survived by his widow, who still operates the store in Santa Cruz. They had no children.

The fact that In the Midst was a journal, an in-process work, rather than a finished product makes it easier to observe the process of Bell's changing thoughts and the process of creativity. An aspect of the creative personality is the ability to fantasize.[24] Bell demonstrates this ability over and over in the book about his last illness. He tries many times and in many ways to imagine his own death and then to verbalize it. About half-way through the book, he adverts to these various attempts and why he is making them.

> I've likened death to sleep, to the unconsciousness of anesthesia, to a wall blocking my further path, to a soft darkness, but it has been a traffic in figures of speech. The thing itself has always eluded me. And it is . . . death itself, I should like to capture, if only for a moment. It would take me no longer than that to see death plain, find the right words to describe it and then let it go, my curiosity satisfied. . . .
>
> And if I could imagine and believe, what difference would it make? . . . it might, once and for all, help me comprehend the reality and inevitability of my approaching death, and thus make me better able to deal with it. . . . to . . . transcend it, master it, and if that isn't possible, then to remain up to the last moment master of myself.[25]

Further on, he evolves another solution:

> this very inability [to imagine what death is like] is itself but a foretaste of death. Not to have a mind is to be dead? To be unable to imagine anything is death? Yes, that I can understand.[26]

Other aspects of the creative personality are earnestness, dedication, and a feeling that one is called to the task of giving some truth to one's fellow men. Writers and other artists, research has indicated, are far from the flighty or bizarre creatures of popular belief.[27] Bell's dedication to his task is shown by the writing he did during his painful and fatal illness. His earnestness is suggested by the fact that, his wife writes, "he always had pen and pad on the night table and many a night, he'd sit up and write notes."[28] His vocation to tell the truth as he saw it is indicated by his discussions of America, its faults, and its possibilities in his novels and autobiography.

Discussion of work

Thomas Bell wrote that his first novel *The Breed of Basil* (1930) was much influenced by Cabell's *Jurgen*, but any reader of such things as *The Three Musketeers*, *The Prisoner of Zenda*, and other stories laid in various Ruritanias could have created a similar melange of medieval, Renaissance, and Victorian periods and settings. Even though the swords, banners, pageantry, and other chivalric flourishes never quite ring true, Bell's later, truly realistic work is foreshadowed by details that are well done--the taste of coffee, how cold eggs look on a plate, and how window shoppers look as they pass in front of a bookstore.

Bell had a feeling for language, a fascination for individual words and how they could be manipulated and combined.[29] A careful reader who also has a feeling for words and some experience in analyzing literary styles can witness Bell play with words, phrases, and styles in Breed of Basil and enjoy his later discussions of words and their uses in In the Midst of Life. To take the style of this novel apart and point out where Ruritanian artifice ends and realistic writing begins would be an interesting exercise in nuance, but a far too detailed process for the purpose of this study.

Even though Breed of Basil is a poor novel, the detailed descriptions of homely things and the feel for language tell the sensitive reader that a talent is here. Bell's art grew steadily from this apprenticeship to his master work Out of This Furnace, declined slightly in Till I Come Home Again, and flourished again in There Comes A Time. In the matter of content, also, it is important to note that Bell wove serious concerns into conversation between his swashbuckling hero and other characters, a technique he used again in his later books. Some of these concerns were love and marriage, religion, the meaning of life and death, and the purposes and functions of literature.

In his second novel The Second Prince (1935), Bell repudiates the historical romance as a genre for him, even though the title might suggest otherwise. (When this novel was published in England, it was named Striker Godown after the main character.) In this novel, Bell begins to utilize his own experiences in his fiction. Striker Godown is a young man of the middle class, but he comes from a mill town in Pennsylvania and many of his adventures parallel those of Bell himself.

Striker had left his home to find adventure, beauty, and truth; he finds, instead, hard work and poverty. Striker works as a laborer and ships out on freighters several times. When he has had his fill of the hard life of a worker, he spends a night with Lee, the girl of French-Canadian and Italian descent he has loved for a couple of years. He cannot commit himself to her, though, because he feels he must return home to integrate and evaluate what he has learned on his adventurings, and to decide what to do with his life. He does not want to sell his life eight hours a day in order to live the rest of the day, nor does he want to sell out to power structures now that he has seen their heartlessness and corruption from the point of view of a worker.

When he goes home to Jericho, a mill town on a river, he has a chance to become editor of the local paper by marrying the wealthy girl who owns it. He does not want to seize this opportunity to enter the power structure at least until he organizes his life according to his new values.

The middle portion of the novel describes his encounters with the upper middle class old-stock Americans of his past and the judgments he forms of them. He finds the men and women of his own age more or less content to be what their class has molded them to be. Older persons, he finds, try to make him conform to those same molds and to pacify his doubts and yearnings with conventional wisdom.

Striker is the "second prince," however; the prince in the fairy tale whose story is never told, he says, the one who goes adventuring on unworn paths, against tradition and against conventional advice. He wants to take those unworn paths, to live a life flecked with beauty and happiness. He wants to live consciously, to be a rebel, a "striker."

In this novel, Bell is working with two symbols for his hero: the "second prince" metaphor to indicate non-conformity, adventurousness, and rebellion; the name "Striker" carries the meaning of fighter along with adventurousness and rebellion. Striker's friend Mike Strovenik calls striking steel workers "the only adventurers in the world today."[30] Striker expands on this idea:

> Most people are weak, cowardly; they sigh and make the best of things. The brave man, the rebel, the adventurer, fights. When I see a striker I feel like tipping my hat. Yes, the dirty little men and women with placards on their chests marching up and down before a factory or store. Poorly dressed, foreign-looking, decidedly unattractive--but they're braving ridicule, starvation and jail to fight for their ideals.[31]

Never again did Bell use quite such obvious symbolism of title or name, or go to such lengths to explain them.

In this book, as in Breed of Basil, the descriptions of middle class homes, furnishings, dishes, and dinner parties do not ring true. However, Mike Strovenik and his life do have the ring of authenticity: parts of Bell's own life and beliefs became Mike Strovenik. Two very clear parallels between Mike and Bell are attitudes toward religion and toward the uniqueness of the individual. In telling Striker about the life of the workers in River Street and the waste of human beings there, Mike says, "God has nothing to do with it. . . . I've always considered River Street incontrovertible proof that God did not create the world."[32] Six years later, Bell has Mike Dobrejcak in Out of This Furnace speak the same thoughts and even some of the same words:

> Once I used to ask myself, Is this what the good God put me on earth for, to work my life away . . .? I couldn't believe it. Now I know that God had nothing to do with it. . . . For there is no God and it doesn't matter how we live or when we die.[33]

Speaking as himself in his last book, Bell writes that he knew in his early twenties that "there was no God and that religion was evil. I'd known it for years."[34]

Mike Strovenik tells Striker that it was not fair to be deprived of a better life, because "When I was born the world began. When I die the sun will go out" and he refers to himself as "this unique Me, this amazing and never to be seen again Me."[35] It was in 1935 that Bell gave these words to a character who was the son of a Slovak laborer, and he himself was thinking those same thoughts twenty-five years later. In In the Midst of Life he writes, "When I was born the world began, when I die the world will end. We come back to that."[36] Striker had met Mike while working in New York City, where he had gone by the name of "Strove." Upon hearing that Mike was back in Jericho, Striker goes to find him in the First Ward, on River Street near the steel mill. One of the things he sees in Mike's room is a desk. There is a similar desk in Out of This Furnace, where it serves as an important symbol of striving for a better life. Mike had been a union organizer in New York, and he does organize a strike in Jericho, but the outcome is left unresolved in this book.

Mike has returned to River Street, he tells Striker, "in search of beauty" even though River Street is "poor and mean and ugly." He speaks of poverty, of being

> cheated, denied the very food and rest my growing body needed. When you reach sixteen in River Street you have working papers and a lunch bucket thrust into your fist and off you trot to the Iron Works or the glass house or Mr. Stewart's carpenter shops. At fifteen or fourteen if your parents don't mind perjury.[37]

He is bitter against Americans who do not recognize his Slovak people as fellow humans, who treat them as part of the profit-making mechanism of their companies, as he tells of the young men and women still living in River Street, destined to

> die criminals and murderers, . . . whores and dipsomaniacs. And they, mind you, will be the best of River Street, the ones with courage to break away, try for something better. . . . But what equipment has River Street given them? Malnutrition and disease are rotting their bodies just as the old-maidish lies of the world's greatest educational system are rotting their minds.[38]

Mike speaks of his own life, contrasting it with the middle-class existence on Indian Hill where Striker lives, explaining by implication why he has become a radical and a union organizer. What follows is an evocation of the lives of the Slovak immigrants and their children, victims of poverty and prejudice. It is one of the parts of The Second Prince that rings true and one of the most clear-cut portrayals of ethnic status that any of the authors in this study allowed himself. Here are details of the early life of Thomas Bell and here in embryo is Out of This Furnace and the union activities of the protagonists of that novel and two later ones.

The children of River Street, Mike says, had good times when they went berry picking and swimming, but even at those moments, their pleasure was tainted by the knowledge that there were shortcuts they could not take, because they were not welcome in Indian Hill, the neighborhood where the "Americans" lived.

> Though we had been born here we were foreigners, hunkies, polacks. We lived in the First Ward, we could jabber in a language other than English, our names were funny and impossible to spell and pronounce. You can have no idea what it meant. A sensitive child lived in hell. He couldn't protect himself, he had no defense against the contempt and ridicule which was directed against him, his foreigness [sic]. As if born a cripple one was constantly taunted with it, made fun of.[39]

Mike questions what America had given these "foreigners." It had taken away the traditional lullabies and replaced them with popular songs. It had taken away the traditional religious holidays and most of their accompanying home rituals and replaced them with "paper hatchets and colored pumpkins and firecrackers." He gives an example:

> "When my mother had a holiday she went to church and prayed. She scrubbed and cooked and baked. The very food she ate on that day had some particular significance; the bread was shaped so, there were meats and cheeses you got at no other time."[40]

He makes a bitter contrast between those and the Americans' "precious holidays":

> "[They] were--to us--days when the banks closed and the mills shut down and there was less than usual in the pay envelope, days when there was bunting in the school auditorium and all the girls had to wear white dresses and Col. Shoemaker made a speech about something which we assumed must be very interesting to Americans but which we did not understand at all, though we applauded politely and sang as much as we could of the 'Star Spangled Banner' and our parents did not interrupt Col. Shoemaker's speech with remarks about a day's wages lost."[41]

Mike fantasizes an autobiography he would like to write to show Striker and others "a picture of American industry that never gets into the advertising pages or the lives of poor boys who became millionaires."[42] He does not mention here the ethnic heritage of the poor; perhaps it is not necessary to mention it; the plight of the poor is universal, not a thing of nationality. Mike speaks as passionately in this part of his narrative as in the previous part. He names all the great mill towns to indicate that conditions were the same in all of them. He speaks of industrial warfare, of men being "hounded, spied upon, fired, blackballed, locked out . . . beaten, jailed, shot." He recounts injustices such as low wages, evictions, cruel retaliations when someone protested at being swindled out of his pay, and "union leaders selling out their own men. . . . [and] cotton, wheat, thousands of tons of foodstuffs being destroyed while millions go hungry and unclothed." He would depict in his autobiography the results of these injustices:

> "You see men wipe out their own families with gas or bullets because they can no longer hope to feed them.

> You sit near a radio with Mike and a white-faced woman nursing a child and a man with his spine snapped by a policeman's club, listening to the voice of a great, rich man asking the poor to be patient, to trust in America, to share what they have with their neighbor--a spectacle to make God ill. . . ."[43]

Mike then speaks of his marriage, of his wife, their poverty, and how she, exhausted by work and poverty, died in her sleep. Then Mike speaks of his future, the work in the world he has chosen to do, and the place where he belongs, River Street. He is going to get what he wants, and what he wants is

> "Col. Shoemaker's house and clothes and money and power. We're out to build a new world. We'll make our own holidays and train our children to an Americanism that will be something more to them than colored pumpkins and a speech by a ward heeler.
>
> The future is mine. I mean to make things happen. Yes, by God! They got my father, they got my mother, they got my wife. Poverty and over-work spell tuberculosis and death. What can it mean to you when I say my mother worked herself to death to keep her children alive? . . . I saw her on her knees scrubbing floors. I saw her bent over a sewing machine until dawn. I saw her trembling with weariness when she got out of bed in the morning to go wash some one's dirty clothes. I saw her need rest and milk and eggs and the stores full of them and her dying because she hadn't money to buy them. I saw it with these eyes, day after day."[44]

The chapter ends with this comment, "Revolutionaries, Mike had said, were not born. They were made."[45] There is no way for the reader to decide whether this comment should be attributed to Striker or whether it is Thomas Bell's own thought.

If Breed of Basil was the rather poor first effort of a young man trying to become a writer, Second Prince is a catharsis:

the delineation of that young man's own life melded into an effort to describe American society as he saw it and felt it. At the end of this novel, Bell's protagonist, Striker, says that he must become a writer of the present, of reality, of what he knows. He had been working on a novel about a romantic incident in the past of his family but decides to abandon it, realizing that he cannot sustain interest in the past; he is a radical and must write about the present. His feelings are reinforced by the opinion of Mike Strovenik that words "are nothing in themselves. . . . It's what they make you do. . . . It's what a word makes you do you want to look out for."[46]

This novel is the actual working out of the manifesto that Striker speaks to himself and Lee at the end, saying that he wants "to write for his own day and neighbors; . . . to leave his mark on his world as it had left its mark on him."[47] His aspiration receives reinforcement from Mike, who has written him that "we can use scribblers too" in the workers' movement.[48]

At the end of the novel, Striker has married Lee and left Jericho. He has found himself as a man and as a writer, and he realizes that he must continue to seek truth and a richer, more principled life, leaving behind neutrality, detachment, and his observer stance. He must become a writer who fights in the workers' cause, trying to reshape the world and recover people's souls for them.[49]

The work that Bell--portrayed as Striker--learned he must do was to integrate his own experiences and attitudes and transmit them in his fiction. Bell had taken his lunch bucket in his fist at fifteen; he had traveled the world and tried many trades. Now he had found the work he would do for fifteen years.

The things Bell had seen and known form the only authentic aspects of _The Breed of Basil_. He brings more reality to _The Second Prince_ in the character of Mike Stovenik and in the solution to Striker's quest for identity and purpose.

Bell's next two novels are the mature products of the experiences and feelings he began to write about in _The Second Prince_. Striker Godown spoke of the struggle to write well and truly. _All Brides Are Beautiful_ (1936) is the fruition of Bell's struggle; it accurately and sympathetically portrays what it was like to be unemployed and on the edge of poverty during the Depression of the thirties. This story of the first two and a half years of the married life of Peter Cummings and Susan Allis is full of hope and charm, however, because of the freshness of their experiencing of each other. _All Brides Are Beautiful_ is the portrayal of a marriage as it grows and shapes the partners. It depicts growth on many levels--emotional, sexual, political, and intellectual.

Leslie Fiedler has stated in _Love and Death in the American Novel_ (1960), "Our great novelists . . . tend to avoid treating the passionate encounter of a man and woman, which we expect at the center of a novel."[50]

Perhaps, then, the work of Thomas Bell should become better known. All Brides contradicts Fiedler's thesis; Bell narrates the deepening of Peter and Susan's love as they live together, build up little rituals, understand one another more, and help each other to be more fully human.

The main theme of All Brides is hinted at in the title. As Susan and Peter discuss whether they should get married, Susan says, "All brides are beautiful."[51] Her meaning is that the wedding day is full of hope, the bride is beautiful in her happiness and eagerness for life, but that the drudgery of housekeeping, the weariness of child-bearing and child-rearing, and the possible dwindling of the husband's interest, which might include physical cruelty and philandering, all these things--in the passage of time --make a woman not beautiful.

The marriage of Susan and Peter, however, makes Susan more beautiful, because she learns her identity through his reflection of her. Peter is the central intelligence of this novel, so his analysis of the marriage is the one the reader receives; his view of Susan is the one the reader shares. Through their relationship, Susan matures, becoming more of a person and more of a woman. Peter learns differences in the ways men and women see things, feel things, and react. But he also learns that there are similar needs and feelings. He learns that men sometimes criticize women for needing reassurances, for wanting certain things and doing certain things. After some self-analysis, he realizes that these are human needs, not merely feminine needs. Thus, he, too, grows more understanding and more fully human because of this relationship. Fiedler has also stated that American novelists "rather shy away from permitting in their fictions the presence of any full-fledged, mature women, giving us instead monsters of virtue or bitchery, symbols of the rejection or fear of sexuality."[52] Susan is only the first of the mature women that Bell portrays; the relationship between Susan and Peter is only the first of the sensual, emotional, and intellectual relationships he describes. His men and women neither fear nor reject sexuality.

All Brides is a realistic novel: It deals with lower middle class (or working class) people; it presents many small details of furniture and other artifacts in the home and at the machine shop where Peter works, and of daily routines. Leo Gurko discusses Bell in The Angry Decade (1947), including him among such proletarian writers as Steinbeck, DiDonato, Edward Dahlberg, and Thomas Maltz. He says Bell is "concerned with workers, but their political views end with trade-unionism and anti-fascism,"[53] indicating that Bell was not a proletarian writer in the strict socialist realism definition of that term.

He notes that Bell "has a talent for making his characters live and for getting them to talk idiomatically and convincingly." He mentions that Bell's novels are "nearly always small-proportioned and on a minor scale" and "cameoed" with skill. His comment on All Brides is that the events in the novel are familiar ones but that

Bell describes them with "surprising freshness."[54] After discussing Bell's two subsequent novels, he concludes that "proletarian literature as a movement has had a fermenting influence upon him."[55]

All Brides borders on the naturalistic, also; the characters are at the mercy of outside forces: the Depression and unemployment. They endure a soul-shriveling suppression of needs and all the emotional strains caused by that suppression within each person and in relationships. It is not totally naturalistic, however, because Peter and Susan and some of the other characters do not react as pawns of fate; they practice petty swindles as well as petty economies. They also try to better their lives; Peter takes drawing lessons, endeavoring to enter the world of book illustration. Susan's sister and brother-in-law try to better their home situation in several ways.

Peter had come to New York City in his early working years without his family. He is a machinist, but he loses his job soon after he and Susan are married. When he does obtain a new job after about two years, he works nights, so he and Susan must make an adjustment in their pattern of life; this adjustment is painful, because they can be with each other only for a few moments before she goes to work in the mornings and on weekends.

Peter is a Communist, but he confines his activities to reading The Daily Worker and marching in the May Day parade. Throughout the major portion of the book, he does not go to Communist meetings nor associate with other Communists, nor does he propagandize except in an occasional conversation with his in-laws. At the very end of the book, as he becomes acquainted with some of his fellow workers in the shop, he begins to notice who reads The Daily Worker and propaganda flyers being distributed in the plant, and he begins to feel out these men with the idea of starting some concerted action.

The novel ends with Peter and Susan planning a little anniversary celebration; none of their economic problems is solved, and their future is uncertain, but the final note is not one of despair or discouragement but of youthful hope.

All Brides Are Beautiful does not have an ethnic dimension. The vaguely WASP names betray no particular nationality group, nor do words, foods, or customs suggest any ethnic background. Bell explores many facets of marriage and man-woman love, using Susan and Peter and the other couples in Susan's extended family to do so. This novel is about depression living, what joblessness and near-poverty can do to working men and their families, about love and marriage, but not about ethnicity nor Americanization. There are criticisms of American society and how men must sell their lives in order to live, but these are from the point of view of the industrial worker, not necessarily the son of an immigrant.

Five years after this novel came Bell's masterpiece Out of This Furnace (1941), the saga of three generations of Slovak steel workers. Of all the books read for this study, this novel most clearly and fully portrays the immigrant experience.

Lebedeff's The Heart Returneth delineates the problem of Americanization quite clearly, but her novel covers only a brief span in the lives of her characters; Mangione's Mount Allegro portrays two generations of Italians, but if poverty and prejudice touched his family and their neighbors, Mangione chose not to treat these stern aspects of life.

In Out of This Furnace, however, Bell created an extended family and their friends and described several neighborhoods over a span of three generations. He portrayed the hardships of the immigrant life, the struggles of the second generation, and the partial successes of the third. His arena is the steel mill towns around Pittsburgh; his concern is with poverty, conditions in the mills, how these hardships affect men and women, and with the waste of lives and talent. He portrays changing relationships between men and their women generation by generation. He expresses his own hope for the betterment of these families and for all Americans, and for a more free and more fully human life for both men and women. As Gurko says,

> Bell stepped out of the small canvas in which he had hitherto functioned so well. . . . Himself of Slovak origin, he defines the speech and the psychological nuances of his immigrant characters with a rare sense of intimacy.[56]

Each of the four parts of Out of This Furnace focusses on the life of one person (who is its central intelligence), but these lives are linked by blood or marriage. Djuro (George) Kracha, a Slovak, came alone to America from Hungary in 1881, leaving behind his wife, mother, and sisters. He comes to work with his brother-in-law, Andrej Sedlar, on a railroad track gang in northern Pennsylvania and follows him when he goes to work in a steel mill in Pittsburgh. Joe Dubik, the first person that Kracha meets in the United States, also works on the track gang. He and his wife Dorta also go to Pittsburgh. These three men, their wives and children and grandchildren constitute an extended family throughout the novel, living near each other in the little towns around Pittsburgh, struggling to achieve a better life, dying in accidents or from diseases of the poor, and sometimes giving in to bitterness.

Kracha feels America only as a different job; he has to struggle just as hard to make his living in America as in the old country. He sends for his wife; they have children, but the years are not kind to them nor, for the most part, to their children. The only period of near-prosperity he has is when he leaves the mill and becomes proprietor of his own butcher shop.

At this time, also, he has an extramarital fling with a woman he had met on the boat coming from Europe. When his wife dies, he marries this sexy widow but his happiness and prosperity are short-lived. The widow is secretly fleecing him, many debts come due at the same time, and he loses his shop. He goes on a roaring drunk, the widow leaves with his money, and Kracha becomes a boarder in the homes of relatives and friends, never again quite the same exuberant man who came from Slovakia.

Finally, old, bitter, irascible, and somewhat withdrawn, he lives with his grandson. When he dies, an elderly woman at his wake expresses what she and he and many others of their generation must have felt about their life in America.

> In the kitchen Dorta was talking with a woman. . . , a heavy, old woman whose hands lay lifelessly in her lap, whose feet looked like misshapen lumps. She was saying in Slovak, "Who knows better than I? Look at me, look at my hands, look at my feet. That is what America did for me. My husband sent for me and put me in a house and filled it with boarders, and for thirty years that's all I saw of America. Work, work, day and night, cooking, scrubbing, washing. And now I can hardly walk, I can hardly put a spoon to my own mouth. They told me, Oh, you're going to America, that's a fine place, you'll live enough for two lives there." Her face was old and tired and resigned. "And I have, I have."[57]

Mike Dobrejcak is the central intelligence of the second part of the novel. He had come to America as a boy of fourteen and began working in the steel mill. He becomes a man of depth and feeling. He learns to read and write English: he reads the newspapers and follows local politics and the work of unionization in the mines and mills and thereby becomes a man the other men look to for knowledge and advice. A symbol of the difference between Mike and the other working men is the desk that he buys in which to keep important papers and the family Bible.

Mike begins to court Kracha's daughter Mary while she is working as a hired girl for a middle class family, who live on a hill in the better section of town. Once, when he calls for her, the family is not home, and Mary shows him the main part of the house. They dream for a moment of living in a house like it--clean, well-furnished, quiet, and warm. This episode does not suggest the house as a model for their aspiration; it portrays, rather, their realization of the distance between their class and the middle class, the uselessness of hoping to bridge that distance.

Mary and Mike marry and are happy together, but their life is filled with work. He continues at the mill; as their family increases, she takes in boarders to supplement their income until the doctor advises her to cut down on her work. On their oldest son's eleventh birthday, after a celebration with cake and candles, Mike goes to work and is killed--crushed and burned by steel. Here, Bell has taken a tragic event from his own life, the death of his father on his own eleventh birthday, and made it more tragic and more pertinent to his theme of the exploitation of the workers.

Mike Dobrejcak's death at the age of thirty-nine is poignant, because it is unexpected, and because it follows an equally poignant scene of married love and tenderness. Bell's talent is fully mature; he does not have someone relate this tragic incident as he had Mike Strovenik relate his tragedy in _The Second Prince_. He narrates it; he does not have to inject bitterness or compassion. Mike Dobrejcak's unexpected death is a shock to the reader, making him or her share the tragedy and the bitterness of such a needless death.

In one of the few references to his father in _In the Midst of Life_, Bell writes that his father had "used him unfairly" but Mike Dobrejcak in _Out of This Furnace_ is anything but a cruel or unfair man. He is earnest, kind, and loving, and he constantly strives for personal growth and the betterment of his family. It is to him that Bell gives a speech that possibly defines Bell's own motive in writing this lengthy book.

Mike and his friend Stefan Bodnar are on their way home from a tavern. They seat themselves on a stoop, because they are too wobbly to walk, and Mike speaks of their work, their people, and their lives. He says it is a "terrible and beautiful thing to make iron," honest and needed work, for which the workers should be honored. He loves his work and wishes he could take pride in it, but the Slovak workers are not honored, the good that is in them is "never asked for. We're only Hunkies."[58]

Then--thinking aloud more than talking to his friend--he tells of an idea he once had to help the mill bosses and their associates understand the Slovak workers.

> "If we were to sing some of our songs and explain what they were about--would it surprise them to learn that we sang about such things and had such feelings? If we told them how we lived in the old country, how we worked the land, the crops we grew, the little money we saw from one year's end to another, our holidays and festivals--would they realize that even though we spoke different languages we were still men like themselves, with the same troubles, the same hopes and dreams? I hoped we might learn to respect one another, that we might even become friends. And once we were friends it shouldn't take us long to discover that we had the same enemies. . . .
>
> "I used to have such ideas, make such great plans. No more. Once I used to ask myself, Is this what the good God put me on earth for, to work my life away in Carnegie's blast furnaces, to live and die in Braddock's

> alleys? . . . Now I know that God had nothing to do with it. Chance rules the world. . . . For there is no God and it doesn't matter how we live or when we die."[59]

Bell writes that Mike is in "a world-encompassing despair,"[60] and when his friend goes home, "Never in life had he felt so alone."[61] But the author does not leave the reader with despair or hopelessness. He gives Mike's thoughts, his mood and values, and ends with the hope implied in lived ideals.

As he walks on home, Mike thinks of his hatred of "poverty and ugliness," his resentment of injustice, his protest against "the degradation of man by man." He recalls his belief in human dignity and the aspirations he has beyond work and food, which are to him only "the beginning of living." Men should gather

> life's richer fruits, love and pride, laughter, accomplishment, the things of the heart and the head that lifted man above the brute. . . . The world held enough for all and if some had less than others it was because men had ordered it so and it lay in men's hands to order differently. It had seemed to him that men needed only to have this explained to them and they'd rise and do what was necessary; and when they didn't he felt angry and bewildered. . . .
>
> Yet he clung to his belief that the mass of men were in their hearts good, . . . Unless this could be proved true here and now, today, in the teeming alleys and courtyards and kitchens of the First Ward, it was true nowhere, never. And unless it was true there was no hope.
>
> It never entered his mind that he himself was all the proof and hope he needed.[62]

Mike is the proof and hope; he is the link between the first generation of immigrants and the third. He educated himself to know and understand some of America's ideals as well as many of America's shortcomings. His aspirations are unfulfilled at the time of his early death; he does not live to see the triumph of his son, who joins with other steel men and union workers to begin a better future, fulfilling some of America's ideals, repairing some of its failures.

The third section of this novel is the story of Mary's widowhood and struggle to keep her family together. When overwork and poverty break her health, she and her three younger children are sent to a state sanitarium. The oldest son, Johnny, nicknamed "Dobie," who has been working since he was fourteen, stays with relatives. He works in a glass factory, in an electric shop, and on roads, and does any other work he can. When Mary succumbs to tuberculosis, two of the children, Mikie and Agnes, are sent home to live with an aunt. The third, Pauline, stays on in the sanitarium, where she, too, dies of tuberculosis. Mikie becomes a machinist and later moves to New York City. When the banks fail, Agnes loses the insurance money her mother had left her; her boyfriend leaves her. She continues to work at low-paying jobs until she marries an older man.

The fourth part of the book is the story of Johnny's late adolescence and adulthood. He has a brief sojourn in the auto plants in Detroit, where he calls himself "John Dobie" and discovers that "saying you were an American satisfied no one,--where did your father come from?--"[63] He returns to Pennsylvania and marries, involving himself in the work of unionizing the mills. He enjoys this struggle because he begins to feel master of his own destiny. Here is the way he explains it to his wife.

> "Because I got so God damn' fed up doing nothing during the depression. I don't mean work. I mean not being able to do anything about it. The whole country was going to hell and the fat boys that were supposed to know it all just made a lot of noise and looked out for themselves. The rest of us sat around watching our jobs and everything we had getting shot out from under us without being able to do anything. On the level, I think that used to get me down more than anything else. But now we ain't waiting for anybody and anything that happens from now on we're going to have plenty to say about."[64]

Later on, Dobie is talking with his grandfather and their old friend Dorta about a union meeting. The old people remember what Dobie's father had done.

> Kracha took his pipe out of his mouth. "Mike should be sitting here listening to him, eh?"
>
> Dorta smiled. "What did I say when Joe told me he [Dobie] had been elected secretary of the union? Mike, nebosčik, should be alive today."
>
> "If he was," Dobie said, "he'd probably be secretary instead of me."
>
> "He was always saying there ought to be a union. He nearly got into trouble more than once. He was never one for keeping quiet. But he used to say, If I don't speak out it will poison me."[65]

The CIO men who come to help the steel workers organize teach Dobie a great deal about unions and about politics and show him that America can be made into the country it should be. When Dobie remarks to one of them, "If a union ever gets into the mills it'll have to go into politics,"[66] the union organizer gives him a more basic political point of view.

> "Let me tell you something a lot of people never realize. If you're making a living in this country you're in politics whether you think so or not. People who never vote or say it's a racket and things like that are simply getting the other guy's politics, that's all. The smart people go out and make their own."[67]

Dobie goes to Washington with some other union men from the steel plant to testify at a Labor Board hearing. As he watches and listens to the lawyers from both sides--the companies and the union--Dobie feels that the hard truth is being covered over with words or misunderstood by people who have never worked as he and his people have.

The witnesses, like himself, "were awkward, their clothes didn't fit, they perspired and used bad grammar" but they and their people, he felt, should be the Board to sit in judgment, or, he muses, there should be

> a jury of ghosts: Mike Dobrejcak and Mary and Pauline, Joe Dubik and Kracha--the maimed and the destroyed, the sickly who died young, the women worn out before their time with work and child-bearing, all the thousands of lives the mills had consumed as surely as they had consumed their tons of coke and ore. They would have known what the words meant. They would have known what was being fought for here.[68]

At the very end of the book, the fight for the union is won, and Dobie and his wife are expecting their first child. He ponders these events and their meaning. He feels that he has become a man and an American, even though the epithet "Hunky" will still be hurled at him. He will still wince at the word and feel deprived and diminished, yet not with the sense of humiliation and bitterness that the epithet had once given him. For he knows he has achieved goals he can be proud of; he is sure of his own talents and powers; and he can even understand that it is ignorance and meanness which make people cling to epithets like "Hunky."

He recalls that the steel towns had always defined "American" as white, Protestant, middle-class, Anglo-Saxon, but now he feels that the CIO men are the real Americans, whatever their nationality. They did not come over on the Mayflower nor talk much about Americanism and patriotism, but they lived their values and practiced integrity.

He realizes that he--like the steel he helps make--has "Made in the U.S.A." stamped on him.

> I'm almost as much a product of that mill down there as any rail or ingot they ever turned out. And maybe that's been part of the trouble. If I'm anything at all I'm an American, only I'm not the kind you read about in history books; . . . anyway, not yet. And a lot of people don't know what to make of it and don't like it. Which is tough on me but is liable to be still tougher on them, because I at least don't have to be told that Braddock ain't Plymouth Rock and this ain't the year 1620.[69]

He continues to think about what America means to him, what he has fought for and will continue to fight for, and what he wants for his son. Equality before the law, freedom of speech, self-respect, integrity, the dignity that all human beings should be allowed, the right to live the way one wanted until one wanted to change that way--all these are what America means to Dobie.

Out of This Furnace is a book about progress; progress accomplished and progress still to come. It is about men from Slovakia who wanted a better life, their children who envisioned that life, and their grandchildren who achieved some of that vision. Kracha and his generation lived among their families and countrymen and worked such long hours that almost any activity except the most necessary--eating, sleeping, and working--was impossible.

Kracha's daughter Mary went to grammar school and participated in the life of the middle class through her work as cook and maid. Mike, her husband, remembered what was good in his homeland and yearned for a better life in his adopted country. He passed on his vision to his son, John, even as he passed on his desk. Dobie treasured this desk through all the hard times, and when he began to make his father's visions a reality, he used his father's desk to hold the records of the union's activities.

Kracha had taken no part in the Homestead Strike of 1892. Not realizing the importance of striking, he had moved to another town, changed his name, and got a job in another mill. The union was crushed, so that in the time of Mike Dobrejcak, only the most hidden of organizational work could be carried out. But Dobie and his generation of steel workers fought the company, organized themselves, and succeeded in getting the CIO into the Pittsburgh mills. His triumph is the triumph of the working man against the rich and powerful, against those who treated men as parts of the steel-making process and not as flesh and blood. To Dobie,

Americanization is the awakening of men to their dignity as men, to participation in the decisions which shape their destinies.

The characterization of women in *Out of This Furnace* is vivid and compassionate as it is in Bell's other novels. An example is Dorta: although she is not one of the main characters, she is a "full-fledged mature woman" (to recall Fiedler's term), a woman of strength and solid common sense, kindness, and in her mature years, wisdom, also. *Out of This Furnace* is a larger arena than the scope of Bell's other novels, and he is therefore able to portray women of three generations and the changes that occur in those generations. Growing autonomy for women is symbolized by attitudes toward sexual relations. Kracha is lusty, almost animalistic. His wife is a submissive participant in what she considers a necessary, unpleasant part of a woman's duty. Mike Dobrejcak enjoys sex more than Mary does, but she is more sensual than her mother had been. Mary's caution in lovemaking is partly based on her fear of having another baby, because of their poverty and the hardships imposed by extra mouths to be fed. The last scene in which Mike and Mary are together is a beautiful evocation of the love of two people who have been married and who have suffered and laughed together for a dozen years. Mike and Mary are compassionate as well as passionate, companions as well as lovers.

Dobie and his wife are frankly sensual creatures who enjoy each other sexually and in many other ways. She is not a liberated woman by the standards of the seventies, but she is the forerunner of those who are. Dobie confides his plans and aspirations to her; she urges him to continue his struggle, never putting her own concerns before those of the workers.

If Thomas Bell was Dobie, the apprentice electrician and machinist, he was also Mikie, who went to New York. He had left the mills and machine shops to become a writer, but he did not lose his identification with the working class. He used his writing to show the improvements needed in the lives of the workers and how some of those improvements could be achieved. In this novel, he wrote of his own Slovak people: he sang the songs of Mike Dobrejcak.

After this master work, Thomas Bell returned to writing about working class persons of no particular nationality. Till I Come Back to You (1943) is a short, almost slight, novel of one day in the life of Miley Brooks, his girlfriend Sally, and the Bridges family with whom he had previously lived. Miley will leave the next day to begin his Army service; he arranges with Hannah Bridges to invite Sally to the usual Bridges Sunday get-together, so he can seek a reconciliation with her.

Miley and Sally had gone together for some months and then had split up, neither quite knowing why. During the day in which the entire action of the novel takes place, Miley and Sally discuss their relationship and their values, realize they love and need each other, and become engaged. Bell portrays this man-woman love relationship in a humorous, sensuous, deeply human way, as he handled such relationships in his other books.

The working out of this relationship is not the theme of the novel, however; Bell is, rather, portraying the difference between persons who ponder the meaning of life and those who focus on lesser values. Miley is the central intelligence, so the reader is given his thoughts, opinions, and ideas, but Sally shares many of his concerns. In their conversations, they discuss their ideas and their feeling that each of them must play a part, no matter how small, in making the world better. Miley's attitudes center around his wish not to waste the only life he will ever have.

The Bridges group--parents, son, married daughters, sons-in-law, and the single daughter and her boyfriend--are not thinking people nor do they thirst after justice or a better society. They are very human in their Sunday-family-quarrelsomeness, but Bell gives each member of the family a concern for one thing. Each of them is, then, a symbol of one attitude toward life or one value system. These symbolic meanings are quite obvious.

One wonders if Bell did not trust his readers to grasp the meaning or if literary criticism has progressed to such an extent that readers are more sophisticated now. In either case, Bell provides an explanation when he has Miley contrast his own view of life with those of members of the Bridges family. He is speaking to Sally.

> "You can get awfully tired of fighting," Miley said. . . . "Because the fact is, you don't have to do any fighting at all if you don't want to. You can let it lick you, the way it's licked Old Man Bridges. Or you can get enough of what you want to keep you satisfied,

> like Dave. Or you can sell out for any favors that might get thrown your way, like Eddie. Or you can never even realize there's a fight going on, like Nick. You have a choice. And I guess the only reason you don't take an out like that is because you happen to be the kind of guy you are. I can't think of any other reason. And being the kind of guy you are you can't live with your eyes closed, or pretending that something makes sense when it doesn't."[70]

When this book was made into a play, The World's Full of Girls, the point that I find so clear was missed by Nunnally Johnson, who adapted it for the stage, and by all the critics who reviewed it. As the play came across to the critics, it was a love story tacked on to a day in the life of a more or less interesting family. One critic, for example, Herrick Brown of the New York Sun thought that the producer was trying to make the Bridges family into an imitation of the madcap Sycamore family of You Can't Take It With You.[71] In the novel, it is clear that each member of the Bridges family serves as a foil for Miley and Sally. The day with the Bridges gives Miley an opportunity to see himself and Sally juxtaposed against the values of the members of the Bridges group. Even though Bell is not portraying an ethnic group in this novel, there is modeling. Both the older and younger generations of Bridges are all negative models for Miley: they show what he does not want to be. He is a better man and a more concerned American than any of them.

The love story is not tacked on to this display of false and true value systems. Miley and Sally love each other and become reconciled because of their shared values.

The tone of Till I Come Back to You is too patriotic for a reader of the seventies, but it was appropriate for the climate of World War II.

A biographical link to Bell's own life is that he had lived with a family named Gilday for a time. He refers to them as "a synthetic substitute" for a family "like the bread they sell in supermarkets."[72]

Thomas Bell's last novel There Comes A Time (1946) is a mature work, summing up all the social themes of Bell's other fiction from the point of view of a mature protagonist. Joel Pane, the central intelligence of this novel, is forty years old when the story opens; he has come to the time when he begins to feel he is getting old, that his life is a sterile routine, and that he is perhaps wasting his life and powers in the "getting and spending" of daily life, in the world that is "too much with him" and yet not molded or conquered by him.[73] He embodies Bell's mature values as Striker Godown, Mike Dobrejcak and his son Dobie, and Miley Brooks embodied them as these values were maturing. Joel Pane wants to enjoy a more deeply felt and more richly lived life; he is concerned with the progress of all men toward such an ideal life and he wants to know the meaning of any one person's attempt to understand life, to be happy, and to deeply live.

The plot concerns Joel's efforts to unionize the employees in the bank where he works and how these efforts develop his personality and change his life. This small episode in the labor movement, Bell suggests, is only a part of the great changes that are occurring in the world. Bell contrasts Joel, who is part of those changes, with the people who are not.

> A few welcomed change, and a few knew why; such men as Joel. . . . were the happiest. The unluckier . . . resisted and fought without knowing what they were fighting. They gave it many names--the C.I.O., un-Americanism, Communism--but never the right name, which was Change. It made them unhappy; . . . It drove the timorous to embrace the feet of the idol Security, to abase themselves there in a surrender that left them drained of shame; it sent some flying to havens where the old patterns remained as yet undisturbed; it discovered the mercenary in the clerk and put him to ranging his homeland for such pay and glory as he could come by; it broke a few.
>
> And changed them all.[74]

Joel Pane is the head teller in a branch of a large New York bank. He is married and has two children. He is of Slovak ancestry, having changed his name from Panek to Pane when he came to New York from Braddock, Pennsylvania as a young man. Joel's extended family is his wife's sisters and brothers and their families. Bell considers him a member of the working class, so the focus in this novel, as in Bell's other works, is on the life style of that class and how some workers attempt to improve that life. The main action of <u>There Comes A Time</u> is Joel's part in the unionization of his fellow employees. The workers want better pay and better working conditions, but only some of them are willing to admit that bankers are not really different from other workers and must take the same steps to obtain benefits as blue collar workers do.

Engaging in this union activity makes Joel ponder his values and how they came about. In looking back over his life, he thinks of his schooling in Braddock, and the unreality of it. The America he knew then and the one he knows as an adult are not the America he was taught about.

> They had taught him about far countries and the dead past, and let him learn about Braddock and the present for himself. In a western Pennsylvania steel town, during the early years of the twentieth century, children whose playground was the streets, whose adventures were hopping freights and stealing coal, were given an education based on an idealization of the New England farm life of a century before, in the language of the British middle class.[75]

Joel Pane's memories are echoed in Michael Novak's <u>The Rise of the Unmeltable Ethnics</u> in 1971, providing a sad comment on American education.

> Nowhere in my schooling do I recall any attempt to put me in touch with my own history. The strategy was clearly to make an American of me. English literature, American literature, and even the history books, as I recall them, were peopled mainly by Anglo-Saxons from Boston (where most historians seemed to live). Not even my native Pennsylvania, let alone my Slovak forebears, counted for very many paragraphs.[76]

Through the device of Joel's musings, Bell sets up a contrast between the unrealistic education Joel received as a boy and the real education he was receiving through his union activities. Joel remembers:

> In classrooms looking out on the miserable houses and mean streets of an industrial slum, the rooftops and billowing smoke of the mills, Joel had memorized nonsense about boys who never told lies--apparently their mothers always had enough money to pay the insurance agent--about fractions of men who worked fractions of days on fractions of acres, but never a

> straight twelve hours a day in a mill for seventeen cents an hour.[77]

His final impression was that

> he'd never been taught anything whose accuracy he might be able to check, from his own observation and experience, against the knowledge he was . . . acquiring in the streets and at home.[78]

Union work opens up new areas of observation and experience for Joel. First, he becomes more aware of his own potential for action. His new confidence in his potential is shown to him while he is visiting a fellow employee, from another branch of the bank, whom he had not seen for a number of years.

> He was sitting in an ugly little living room, talking to two middle-aged and unprepossessing people who frightened easily. He felt himself growing; if only because they were frightened and he was not; he felt himself larger than they--someone come in from where the fresh winds of the world were blowing, imperturbably at ease with dangerous forces.[79]

In trying to convince people to join the union, he learns much about human nature. Courage, determination, and group loyalty are shown by those who work hard to organize the union. Apathy is shown by those who do nothing; fear by those who sneer and try to undermine the work of the organizers by starting a company union.

When Joel endeavors to explain the worth of the union, he realizes he needs more education to understand the business world and its power base, and the history of America. He feels that scholars, teachers, and preachers had neglected to probe for truth and to promulgate it to those who need to understand the context of their lives. When he and his wife begin political work in their neighborhood, they begin to learn about politics firsthand. They also realize they need more background knowledge about democracy and politics. Nancy begins to read works of the Founding Fathers. When the unionization of the bank is completed, Joel begins to attend night school.

He is asked to speak at a meeting of employees of another bank, who are beginning to consider a union for themselves. He gives them the benefit of his schooling as well as the products of his union experience. He paraphrases deTocqueville by saying, "What a task it is to persuade men to busy themselves about their own affairs!"[80] He tells them that Washington and Jefferson fought for political democracy, but that workers are "fighting for economic democracy."[81]

He defines democracy in action as "people doing things for themselves on their own time."[82] Bell then has him articulate one of the themes of the novel:

> "You'll come out of it [the fight for a union] bigger men and women because you'll have accepted your share of responsibility for making the world a better place to live in. And that seems to me the only job there is these days that's worth all a man can give it."[83]

All the themes of the novel are summed up in a discussion between Joel and his wife Nancy. They consider what would happen if all people could have enough material comforts to live life the way they want in freedom and peace: freedom to grow spiritually, to live deeply, and to pursue the "best use a man could make of his life."[84]

In 1946, then, Bell was expressing the idea that mankind is progressing. His hero, Joel, was a part of Change, and a man who was making change happen. At about this time, Teilhard de Chardin was saying that evolution did not stop with the body and mind of man. In the Chardinian vision, man is progressing from adolescence to maturity just as Bell's bank workers progressed from adolescent fears at the beginning of their organizational work to calm and mature judgment at the end of it. As they took on a greater share of responsibility for making their working conditions better, they found they had potentialities never before given a chance to develop. Chardin, a paleontologist and a theologian, expressed his vision through essays, articles, and books. Bell expressed his vision through the characters he created who saw the development of their own latent possibilities.

Bell explores several personalities whose focus is the acquisition or protection of material things. Several characters Joel knows show in their attitudes how money or lack of it can shape a person's life, how money can change in importance from one time in a person's life to another, and that the means employed to obtain money influences the person making it. For example, Nancy's brother, Richie, who owns a liquor store, is very materialistic, a man who is interested in money-making, getting ahead, and what money can buy for him.

The theme of house-as-soothing-chimera was embodied in Till I Come Back to You in Old Man Bridges and his wife, who were caught in their ownership of a house, always hoping and dreaming of selling it at a profit only to buy another, more suitable, one. A similar theme of property owning the person is treated in There Comes A Time. Joel and Nancy live in an apartment, but they know a couple who own property and are caught up in maintaining it and improving it. Joel thinks there might be some pride in owning and showing off property, but the disadvantages, as he sees them, far outweigh those advantages. He ponders the meaning of these two attitudes.

> Buying one's own home was an American ideal, a veritable passion, and young and old customarily spoke of it in terms less proper to a business transaction than to the solution of every human problem, the sum of attainable felicity. . . . Wrestling with a balky furnace or budgeting one's income to allow for payments . . . might very well take one's mind off less easily solvable problems: the relationship between those problems and the inadequacies of an economic system, for example; the meanness of an existence so spiritually poverty-stricken that it sought (and found) exaltation in an all-electric kitchen, in the fine distinction between paying taxes for the roof over one's head and paying rent for it.[85]

In Bell's work, women are always subordinate to his protagonists, but he is never unaware of the plight and progress of women. In There Comes A Time, Nancy and her sister Maggie become active in neighborhood politicking and later initiate Joel into it. The two union organizers assigned to work with the bank employees are young women, shrewd and knowledgeable, but no less feminine. Some of the men are surprised, some a little disappointed, when the union appoints Milly, a "mere girl in her twenties"[86] to work with them, but she and her successor are experts at their job and gain the respect of all the men.

Nancy is not a full-time activist, as Milly is, but she encourages Joel in his activism in every way. She begins to read the works of Jefferson and Franklin and ponder over American society and her place in it, just as Joel is doing. In a conversation with Joel, she expresses many of the themes of this book in a simple manner: she speaks of politics, of individual responsibility, of education, and of the fleetingness of life.

> I'd love to be doing something like Milly and those other girls down there. . . . I wish I had a lot of time. And a lot of money, so I wouldn't have to worry. . . . I'd read a lot of books and work on committees and get up on my hind legs and broadcast some of the things _I'd_ like to see done. . . . Instead of letting other people run things as though I didn't exist. . . . if you don't bother, somebody else runs things according to their own ideas and then where are you? . . . I went through high school but I'm just beginning to realize I don't know _anything_ about how things got to be the way they are. And you can't improve them unless you know, can you? That's why I wish we had a lot of money. I'd like to buy books and take courses and go to lectures and concerts and art exhibits and things like that. There's so many things we're missing. And we're not going to live forever.[87]

The relationship between Joel and Nancy is rich and sensual. Joel is bored with his life at the beginning of the book and rejuvenated by his union work at the end, but all through the story his relationship with his wife enriches and sustains him. They are never bored with one another. He and Nancy tease each other and frankly appreciate one another's bodies as well as one another's conversation.

Bell explores many man-woman relationships in his novels and portrays many healthy ways that men and women can relate. For example, in this book, Joel loves Nancy's sister Maggie, with a love that is partly sexual, based on her attractiveness as an intelligent, good-looking woman. Both Nancy and Maggie are aware of Joel's feeling; they tease him about it, but Nancy is not jealous, because she understands that this relationship is the appreciation of a good man for a good woman.

Bell also depicts men and women who cannot relate well. An example is Richie, Maggie and Nancy's brother. Even though he is not unhappy with his wife, he has a series of affairs with younger women. Toward the end of the book, when the sisters are discussing their brother's profligacy, they mention that their father had often called him a sissy, but they do not go on and make the obvious Freudian point that Richie's adulteries are his way of constantly affirming his manhood.

There Comes A Time is a novel of progress: one of its themes is mankind's advance through joint action. Women are part of this joint action which makes each person better for the doing of it. Bell delineates a mature man-woman relationship, not as a major theme as in All Brides, but as an intrinsic part of the story.

An ironic postscript to Bell's novels is his short story "The Man Who Made Good in America" (1947). The main character is Mike Dobrejcak, but the "man who made good" is Andy Toth, who had been falsely imprisoned for twenty years for killing a mill foreman in a small riot. After he is found to be innocent, he is released from prison, and the steel company gives him all the pay he would have received in those twenty years.

At the instigation of two cronies, Mike Dobrejcak figures out how much money that would be. It comes to over twelve thousand dollars, and the three steel workers discuss the contrast between Andy Toth's life and their own twenty years of toil and what they have to show for it. Mike pretends to give the speech Toth could give when he gets back to his village in Slovakia, expressing the irony they all feel.

> "My friends, in my youth I went to America to make my fortune, . . . I dreamt of some day returning here rich and famous. Money in my pocket, maybe even my picture in the papers. You all know what thoughts will come into a young man's head when he is going to America. So off I went and now I've come back, and here I am. Rich and famous."[88]

The name "Toth," Bell explains, is a common one; it is a Hungarian word meaning "Slovak." Perhaps Bell means to suggest that all Slovaks were prisoners in America, working their lives away but not ever being rewarded with riches or fame or even comfort.

Conclusion

There is an African folk song about a poor girl who was deceived and exploited by a pimp. The refrain is, "And I holler 'why?' And I holler 'why?' Tortoise Boy no mon amie." It seems to me that Thomas Bell, who was one of the poor, hollered "why?" all through his life and spent his creative talent exploring and answering that question.

The contrasts between poverty and affluence, between American ideals and the reality he knew made Bell desire to change that reality. In his fiction and in his partial autobiography, he wrote of the ideals and the reality and pondered the deeper questions of why some people should be forced to grub their lives away, why society could not assure all people enough freedom from work and worry to develop their personalities fully. His writings depict both the failure of American ideals and the inspiration they can be. He deplored the diminished lives which he saw result from exploitation, commercialism, and capitalism.

He never forgot his origins: he wrote of working class people, for the most part, because he himself was a member of that class and knew firsthand the life of the immigrant and the plight of the poor. He disliked the callousness and arrogance of the rich, their inhumanity and disregard for American ideals--and their privileges. Bell expressed in fiction events and attitudes that Michael Novak, who shared his origins, reported on some twenty-five years later in his social history _cum_ personal polemic, _The Rise of the Unmeltable Ethnics_ (1971). He says, "From 1870 until 1941 ethnics were told they were not worthy of America. They are cynical about authority, but they believed the dream."[89] Further along in the book, he returns to the point, saying that immigrants from southern and eastern Europe "hated many of the inequities of America, but mostly they were trying to keep their families alive and they essentially trusted America."[90]

Bell saw his life in the steel towns as a life of needless suffering. He knew that life for the poor should be better. He saw affluence as a step toward a better life, but he also saw that affluence alone was not the answer, because the affluent often lived a shallower life than his people in Braddock and Munhall had. He wrote of this shallow affluence in the last months of his life, asking of the American that he transcend his environment.

> I want him to be something more than a husband and father and taxpayer, to realize that there is more to life than survival and propagation in ever more expensive surroundings and that the truths and values he presently cherishes waste and demean his life more often than they enrich it. I want him to lift his eyes from his own small world of home and job and take note of the larger world outside, to realize he is a part of it whether he will or no and to accept his due share of responsibility for what goes on in it. . . . I want him to learn the difference between what is best and what is only just good enough. . . . I want him to love all living things, . . . I want him to acknowledge as part of his heritage the obligation to leave the world a little better than he found it.[91]

Gaining a middle class life style was not the answer if it meant losing the songs and traditions, the family life of one's people, the honesty and richness of a growth-relationship between a man and a woman; if it meant concentrating on one's own life and material comforts and taking no responsibility for the country.

Bell did not beatify the life style of the poor or make saints of the working class, as some proletarian writers have done. He saw the virtues of the poor, but he also saw poverty shriveling their humanity. He advocated that workers strive to better the lot of the working class, but he did not portray workers or that striving in simplistic terms. He knew that some workers were unaware of the problems, some were apathetic, some were fearful, some were dishonest or greedy or sensual or acquisitive. He portrayed all of them, but his heroes were men who hollered "why?" and who strove to be better men. They strove in the company of a woman, a family, and a community of workers, with a communal sense that all persons could become better human beings in a better America.

His protagonists are working men, men who wonder about the meaning and purpose of life, because their own lives are spent doing work that has little meaning and no purpose except to buy bread. Some of Michael Novak's very words in his chapter "A Dream of New Work" echo the words of Mike Dobrejcak and Joel Pane:

> What salary is commensurate with the purchase of a man's youth? . . . Why should a man sell eight hours of his energy, five days a week, forty-nine weeks a year--especially if it tears him away from his neighbors, his family, his friends, his own interests and craftsmanship?[92]

Many of Bell's workers are union men, because in concerted action, they feel, there is hope for a more meaningful, richer life. They do not look for models outside themselves, generally, because they are more aware, more thoughtful, and more progressive than those around them. The men and women they know are, for the most part, negative models, i.e., examples of how not to live.

As Bell's protagonists matured, the women he paired with them also matured. In <u>All Brides</u> (1936) Susan was unaware of social problems but became interested through Peter's influence. As noted above, the progress of women in <u>Out of This Furnace</u> (1941)

follows the changes in the men. In Till I Come Back (1943) Sally is as aware of defects in American society as Miley is and speaks of some political activities she had carried out. In There Comes A Time (1946) Nancy is reading Jefferson and Franklin. She thinks through their ideas and her own while she goes about her household chores. Her sister Maggie influences Nancy and then Joel to take part in neighborhood doorbell ringing to get people to register and vote. The two union organizers are young women.

There are apathetic and non-political women in Bell's novels, too, just as there are apathetic and non-political men. But Bell's intent seems to be that all persons must become thinkers, must become aware of the discrepancies between the ideals of America and the actuality, and all must strive to close the gap between ideal and actuality.

Bell does not deal with the Americanization of immigrants in There Comes A Time, Till I Come Back to You, or All Brides Are Beautiful, but he is deeply concerned with the Americanization of America, i.e., the actualization of the ideals of the Constitution and what each American can do to make those ideals a reality.

Only Out of This Furnace is overtly about Bell's Slovak people, but all of his novels deal with the family as a group in contact with other families. And all of them (except the first) deal with groups of workers in conflict with employers. They portray the defects in the structure of American society and the victims who are diminished by those defects. However, the mood of his novels is not depression or bitterness because his characters are so human and rounded, their adventures so homely and hopeful, that the reader has empathy with them and sympathy for the ideals they propose and act out.

In _Out of This Furnace_ Bell treats of the assimilation experience as he portrays three generations of Slovaks from the ocean voyage of Kracha, the immigrant, to the successful union activities of his grandson. The milieu is the extended family, which includes siblings and cousins in the second and third generations, and also the Slovak friends of the grandfather and their children and grandchildren who remain close to his family.

In this three-generation span--from about 1880 to just prior to World War II--these people move upward slightly in income; they are not accepted socially into the mainstream of American life, but they are beginning to acquire power, beginning to make their presence felt as they try to improve conditions in the mills where they work.

Bell deals with the same milieu--the working class extended family--in his other novels, and with the same struggle for a better life, but nationality is not mentioned, and all the characters have Anglo-Saxon names. For the most part, Bell's characters did not model themselves after the Americans they met; rather, Thomas Bell created them as models for other Americans to imitate. His purpose in writing was didactic, not merely descriptive. As Striker Godown says, "Art is propaganda or it is nothing."[93] Now and again, when his characters give too-long speeches or monologues, this teaching function is too obvious. In <u>There Comes A Time</u> and <u>In the Midst of Life</u>, Bell seems to be looking toward the future as well as trying to influence his own day.

Even though Bell used an ethnic milieu only once, his heroes were never the loners of mainstream American fiction. They all had a fiancee or wife who was a real partner in thought and action; and they all had an extended family, relatives, and neighbors, a real social group with which they were in constant contact. Here literary criticism and the theory of ethnic studies meet. Can I posit that Bell wrote <u>always</u> of his own Slovak people--even though they were disguised as Cummings, or Brooks or Pane? He changed Belejcak to Bell, Strovenik to Strove, Panek to Pane; but he did not forget his own childhood in the slums, the poverty, the mouthing of ideals by the affluent and powerful. Nor did he forget the value of love, of relationships, of seeking for what is best.

The self-reliant American who has broken his ties with Europe was an ideal that Ralph Waldo Emerson proffered. The Turner thesis of the lone frontiersman underlies R. W. B. Lewis' Adamic hero, Henry Nash Smith's <u>Virgin Land</u>, and perhaps Oscar Handlin's immigrant--uprooted, alienated, and alone. The newer theory that immigrants lived in groups with communal values is illustrated by the work of Bell, of Lebedeff, and of Field--whether or not they indicate by the family name that their characters are members of ethnic groups.

Bell's hero is a self-reliant man, but he is never alone, just as most immigrants were not alone. He may have broken his ties with many parts of his European heritage, but he did not lose his sense of family nor his sense of group membership. The hero's name may be Anglicized; and his family membership may change from his own blood relatives to a synthetic family or his wife's family; his ethnic group membership may metamorphose into membership in the working class, but he is always a member of a group. He is not an isolato; he is in the thick of American urban, working class life. He wonders "why?" and strives to transcend the worst of that environment "sufficiently to prod the human race another step higher in its long climb from the primeval ooze"[94] as Thomas Bell said in In the Midst of Life.

CHAPTER VII

THE CLIMATE OF CRITICISM AND PUBLISHERS' ACCEPTANCE

Chapter I discussed the place that literary works of all ethnic groups should have in the canon of American literature. The place that any writer has is dependent on many things: first of all, his or her talent as a writer is a *sine qua non*. Other factors are the reviews written by contemporary, workaday critics, the judgment of editors and publishers as to possible markets for a given novel or story, and an intangible "collision," as William Styron termed it, of a particular regional or ethnic sensibility with "a fortuitous time in history."[1]

This chapter will present an analysis of criticism published in newspapers and journals of opinion on the work of these five novelists and then their own thoughts, opinions, and experiences in regard to publishers' acceptance of their work. Most of the novels written by these authors were written in the 1940's; hence, my analysis will be mainly of criticism written in that decade. The criticism written before that generally judges only apprentice works; that after is too scattered to yield a general statement.

Most of the novels were reviewed more than once--in both local and national periodicals, including the New York *Times Book Review*, the New York *Herald Tribune Weekly Book Review*, *The Saturday Review of Literature*, the *New Yorker*, *The Nation*, *The New*

Republic, Time, the Chicago Sun Book Week, the Detroit Free Press, and the Columbus Dispatch. Some of them were reviewed by well-known authors and critics: Jack Conroy, August Derleth, Maurice Hindus, Ben Ray Redman, Edmund Fuller, Benjamin Appel, Clifton Fadiman, Diana Trilling, and Isaac Rosenfeld.

An examination of the responses of these and other critics reveals little insight into the works, or their authors. These critics were, of course, reviewing the books more or less in a vacuum unless they had chanced to read earlier works by the same author. They did not often have knowledge of other books by the novelist whose work they were reviewing or the advantage of knowing the background of his or her life.

Reviewers of the forties did not make use of symbolic analysis, even in such richly symbolic works as The Ship and the Flame, Night Search, or The Heart Returneth. More surprising is the failure of reviewers of Jacob's Son to be aware of the importance of the many references to the work of Chaim Bialik and the "behind the barrel" theme which his work provides. Field explains that this theme is

> crucial to an understanding of Michael's thinking. . . . To Michael bookishness led to cowardice Behind the Barrel. Men must never, never rot Behind the Barrel in time of struggle. And though I should have done more to develop that theme, not a single reviewer even mentioned it![2]

The reviewers of the forties were, necessarily, influenced by the events and attitudes of their time. For example, Ruth Page in her review of No Bright Banner placed it in the context of patriotism in war. She comments, "The question it asks occurs in most current fiction: how does a man feel about the America he is asked to fight for?"[3]

Robert M. Coates, writing in New Masses, praises Ben Field's The Cock's Funeral for bringing "both the techniques and the conventions" of proletarian writing "to harmonious expression," fulfilling the task of the proletarian writer of "establishing new technical fictional cliches that would embody their new conventions of thought."[4]

The political orientation of the forties is obvious in the work of some reviewers. John Norcross, for example, perceived The Heart Returneth as a novel about marginal persons, but he dwelt only upon Prince Lucian, his rejection of the White Russians in America, "the dying embers of a culture already dead," and Lucian's return to the USSR and its "breath of vitality . . . daring hopes and robust creativity."[5] This review was illustrated by a picture captioned "Soviet pilots in a mess tent at a Russian airport."! The reviewer for the Detroit Free Press also concentrated on Lucian; he gave no attention to Andre Borodin and dismissed Anna thus briefly: "Anna Borodin, Andre's twin, achieving success as a dress designer, also slashed away the past, turning to America."[6]

If the reviewers of the 1940's considered the quest for identity as a theme in literature, they judged it always as a positive forward movement; they did not consider that a person could be torn between the half and half identity of the marginal person (attributed to Mangione by Isaac Rosenfeld[7]) for many decades or even a lifetime. Only the most obvious bildungsroman--*No Bright Banner* and *Piper Tompkins*--were perceived as narratives of maturation and identity-search. *Piper Tompkins* is summarized as "a laconic description of a personal awakening in a land of strife" by Nathan A. Rothman in *Saturday Review*.[8]

Mount Allegro was seen as dealing with American identity by only one reviewer, Isaac Rosenfeld, and he hedges his analysis by writing not that Mangione himself had accepted or rejected American identity but that Mangione's "generation has accepted America."[9] J. D. Ross correctly judged *The Ship and the Flame* as a story of a man in limbo between identities as well as between countries, who chooses integrity and action but not a nationality.[10] A better known critic, Edmund Fuller, analyzed it as a novel of ideas rather than an identity struggle. He saw its themes as the isolation of the thoughtful man and the seeming absurdity of hope, but he did not comment on Stiano's clarification of identity.[11]

Ben Field's early novels are treated as regional literature because of their explicit descriptions of farm life and rural towns, not as novels of maturation and personal growth. Moe Miller, Piper Tompkins, and even Michael Berkowitz are judged as unsympathetic characters by some reviewers, who apparently do not remember their own teen years or the silences, sarcasm, and grumpiness of teen-agers rebelling against parental values and mores. One reviewer describes Moe as "a sullen, overdriven adolescent";[12] Nina Brown Baker writes, "Never was there a less glamorous hero than this Moe Miller. He . . . is insensitive to the beauties of nature, he rides roughshod over everything that gets in the way of his job."[13] To Baker, Moe's only redeeming feature is that he "would do all right in the Army. He's good, strong G.I. material for a second front."[14] Rothman refers to Piper Tompkins as "this tough and practically insensitive kid."[15]

Benjamin Appel praises the character Virgil Doggity as "one of the most natural and convincing he-men I have come across in current American fiction. . . . [he] is as real as . . . work." But Appel fails to see the growth in Virge or in The Last Freshet, saying that there was "no dramatic revelation of changing men in an uncertain and changing world."[16]

Bell's works were seen as realistic by most reviewers, notably Frances Woodward, who wrote a very perceptive explanation of Bell's writing. She says Bell has "put two abused, overworked words ['proletarian' and 'realistic'] back into the meaning the dictionary gives them." She explains:

> The proletariat is simply that part of society which never has had much of any money and never expects to have. Realism is the practice of regarding things in their true nature and dealing with them as they are. "All Brides Are Beautiful" is a realistic novel . . . a book about people who live in the Bronx and do not speak in low comedy dialect.[17]

The Second Prince was usually considered derivative and romanticized. E. C. Beckwith, however, praises the lengthy passages given over to discussions by Striker Godown or Mike Strovenik; these are the passages, as I noted above, which foreshadow the later power in Bell's work. These passages, Beckwith writes, give this book "its utmost readability. . . . here familiar truths, theories, ideas are set forth from fresh angles, with new meanings, which one is unlikely to have encountered elsewhere."[18]

Bell's novels were generally well-received, although not universally given high praise. _Out of This Furnace_ was seen as the fine novel it is except by Clifton Fadiman in the _New Yorker_, who saw it as "one of those Americanization chronicles with which we have become perhaps overfamiliar."[19] Margaret Wallace in the New York _Times_ gave _Furnace_ a good review and placed it in the context of Bell's work by noting that the Slovak steel workers in _Furnace_ are "at least the spiritual ancestors" of Peter Cummings of _All Brides_. "It is their tenacity, their long humiliation, their inarticulate pride and anger, their growing sense of Americanism, which produces a Peter Cummings."[20] Wallace was the only reviewer who noted the progress of Bell's work; none of them commented upon the depth of thought or the futuristic elements in his last novel, the elements Bell reiterated in _In the Midst of Life_.

The book with the most lasting acceptance is _Mount Allegro_, which was reprinted for the third time in 1972, in both hardcover and paperback, by the Children's Book Department of Crown Publishers. Mangione's book about Danilo Dolci _A Passion for Sicilians_ was also reprinted last year as a Colophon paperback, now using its former subtitle The World Around Danilo Dolci as its title.

Judgments of editors and publishers as to the feasibility of publishing a given book are based in part on their estimate of the reading (and buying) audience for it. What weight is given to the ethnic composition of that audience is hard to ascertain. Ethnic composition was not considered by Henry Sydnor Harrison in 1914 in his reexamination of the ancient question as to the reasons manuscripts are accepted or rejected,[21] nor by Bernard Berelson in his analysis of the book reading public nearly forty years later.[22]

In 1941 James Laughlin, editor of New Directions in Prose & Poetry made a comment on the book trade in regard to Ben Field's work, but he attributed Field's lack of acceptance to his realism.

> Ben Field is a perfect example of why the American commercial publishing system ought to be housecleaned. There are probably not twenty writers in America today who are better writers than Field, but commercial publishers shun him because, like W. C. Williams, he gives a real picture of life in America instead of a sugar- (or slime-) coated one.[23]

A call for research in publishing was made by Robert E. Cazden in "A Proposed Doctoral Program in Booktrade Research" in 1967, but Cazden does not even allude to the ethnic composition of the American reading public in his exposition of the necessity for such research.[24] The absence of research leaves us with impressions and opinions. In 1971 Allen Guttmann offered an opinion which apparently reflects a common impression among publishers and those interested in the publishing business.

> The audience for most serious books not assigned in classrooms is located largely within twenty-five miles of Times Square. No one knows the precise sociological composition of this audience or the characteristics of the other readers scattered across the nation (frequently in an academic environment) but it is generally assumed that many are secular and Reformed Jews.[25]

I queried the novelists in this study and the widows of Bell and DeCapite about their experiences in getting work published, particularly in regard to the ethnic aspect and the editors' judgments of ethnic groups as possible readers. Mangione supplied a perceptive answer.

> My general impression, both as a writer and as a former publisher's editor, is that publishers will publish anything which they think will sell. If there has been a plethora of Jewish-American books it is simply because a large percentage of American Jews are book buyers. The same cannot be said of Italian Americans. Idaresay [sic] that if there were a larger Italian American reading public, there would be more books about Italian Americans written and more publishers willing to publish them. A book like The Godfather, whose appeal stems from its sensational material, transcends all ethnic boundaries and is purchased by everybody. One of [Mario] Puzo's previous novels, The Fortunate Pilgrim, which deals with Italian American life, had a very poor sale when first published - the same kind of a sale that most novels about Italian Americans have.
>
> One of the earliest bestsellers by an Italian American - perhaps the only one before Puzo and [Gay] Talese - was Pietro Di Donato's Christ in Concrete. But the main reason it sold well was because it was chosen by the Book of the Month Club.
>
> My own book, Mount Allegro, though it has been published four times in thirty years, has had a relatively poor sale. Although it had the renown of a bestseller and was widely acclaimed by the critics, its original sale was less than 10,000 copies. Its total sales to date are less than 18,000 copies and that number includes, of course, two paperback editions.

> I do have difficulty getting any of my fiction published. The Ship and the Flame and Night Search had to be submitted to a number of publishers before they were accepted. I have no difficulty whatsoever, on the other hand, getting my nonfictional material published. Usually, I am able to get a contract for a nonfiction book on the basis of a short outline.
>
> With a book of nonfiction, a publisher thinks he can determine the extent of the market. He can't do that with a novel. And if the novel is about Italian Americans and is not written as a commercial venture, like the Godfather, the guessing becomes all the more difficult since it is a wellknown [sic] fact by now that Italian Americans by and large are not book readers.[26]

Marie Benedetti Bell's answer to my query, "Can you attribute editors' or publishers' reluctance to their analysis of the possible reading audience?" was simply "No."[27]

Natalie DeCapite answered at some length.

> One really outstanding book that hits a spiritual need can start a flood of similar writings - publishers always look for ways to sell books. Like the movies, things go in waves - always intangibles, but mostly one really fine book can start a trend.
>
> We had an awful time getting the first novel published. I don't think Mike had ever heard of an agent at that time - we just peddled it around. Scribner's was such an elegant published [sic], we tried it first. About five - the manuscript was dog-eared, I was working full-time, Mike was going to NYU and not a good typist, we had no money to spare to pay for having it re-typed, so I ironed it out, Mike took it to James Walsh of John Day, got a jacket blurb from Louis Adamic, and that was the beginning. He never was too interested in publishing short things, so they were generally requested.
>
> Publishers want to make money, of course. A prestige publisher will sometimes publish even though the prospect is a poor sales record because it is a prestige author. For a new author, not an outstanding figure of some sort, the type of publisher makes a great difference. An agent knows the markets and is

> generally far more knowledgeable about all this than any writer, but there are faults in the agent procedure too. Mike certainly never would alter anything he had to say or his method of saying it with any commercial idea in mind, because this was not the sort of writer he was.[28]

Mrs. DeCapite also made a comment about markets:

> If I remember correctly Pietro Di Donato's Christ in Concrete came out just before Maria, and since there was such a splash about it we wondered if Maria's sales (not too good) suffered from that - who knows - the reviews were good.[29]

(Christ in Concrete came out in 1938; Maria and Mount Allego were published in the same month in 1943. Mrs. DeCapite may have misremembered which book coincided with the publication of her husband's novel, but her point about sales remains.)

My query asked for an impressionistic answer; the answers were thus quite personal and ranged beyond the work of the novelist. Ben Field was characteristically realistic in his appraisal of the market and of his own work.

> I have had difficulty getting my stories and novels published. Books of short stories are rarely printed. I have a collection of short stories which has been lying on the shelf for years; no publisher will take it. Individual short stories have been accepted by the smaller magazines but I have been unable to get into Esquire--even though the editors have praised several of my Jewish stories, and the reason given was that there were so many Jewish writers at work that the magazine had to be more selective, and by that they meant accepting the work of the TOP NAMES, [sic] only.
>
> The resurrection of Henry Roth's "Call It Sleep" and the emergence of [Bernard] Malamud and Philip Roth and Saul Bellows [sic] and other Jewish writers after World War II indicated that an audience was ready for them. "Call It Sleep" was reprinted in 1960 and the paperback has sold in the hundreds of thousands. The

> others have had a large audience during the last decade and a half. During the forties there was no such audience, I believe, for the writers mentioned above.
>
> When my novel [Jacob's Son] was submitted by my f[r]iend, who happens to be one of the editors at Crown, the attitude was: Another Jewish novel! We were able to convince Crown that my novel was "different", and different it was, but the sales were not anything to dance in the streets or turn somersaults over. Could Crown have done more for it? I don't know. But I should have done more with it, namely, turned out a better novel.[30]

Field's comments on why he wrote for the New Masses and The Daily Worker were included in the chapter on his work. He states that he could "never feel gratitude enough for the opportunities afford[ed]" to him by those two publications and by International Publishers, who issued The Cock's Funeral and the anthology Proletarian Literature in which "Cow" was reprinted. He comments next about his differences with these presses.

> At the same time, I had my difficulties with all three. New Masses turned down "Cow," which Hound & Horn published. I recognized after a while that my chief loyalties were to my integrity as a writer, and that what the Communist Press often insisted on was a carbon copy of reality. There was little room for the creative writer. The worker and the farmer were put on pedestals. Revolution was around the corner. The Red Rooster became a weather cock turning with the wind. Much as I admired my fellow-writers on the staffs of the above periodicals, men and women who worked hard and who had courage and were willing to go to jail for their beliefs, I could not agree with them on esthetic as well as political questions. I stopped writing for the Communist press.[31]

The next question to ask is, "Are we embarked upon what Styron terms a fortuitous time for the ethnic sensibility of the Eastern and Southern Europeans?" There are a few straws in the wind. The reprinting of Mount Allegro in 1972, the publication of The Rise of the Unmeltable Ethnics and the college anthologies which are beginning to include writers from those stocks may portend that such a sensibility is coming to the fore. Italian and Slavic names are beginning to appear on lists of speakers at scholarly meetings and on tables of contents of scholarly journals. These scholars may interest themselves in propagating their ethnic heritage. Ben Field is rejuvenating his career by beginning a new trilogy about American Jews. Mangione has led off G. P. Putnam's new series of juvenile books about ethnic groups.

It takes the perspective of decades to assess the main themes and attitudes of the literature of a decade. In the sixties Eisinger wrote of the fiction of the forties, noting that "the special value of studying the prose fiction of the forties lies in its capacity to expand and deepen our understanding of that time and of ourselves."[32] Perhaps the seventies is the time for greater deepening and understanding through greater awareness of many heritages, many groups that make up our total heritage.

CHAPTER VIII

SUMMARY AND CONCLUSION

The conclusion of this thesis will have to be two-fold: first, a synthesis of the chapters about the five authors and a tentative conclusion about the meaning of their work; second, in light of that conclusion, an essay at a redefinition of American literature.

Each person is the product of his home, his environment, and his early experiences. These five novelists did not escape from these influences even though they were able to go through the looking glass of imagination and shape people and events in the kaleidoscope of creativity. As creative persons, they could fantasize; they could portray events that never happened and people who never lived. Analysis of their work shows, however, much of what happened in their lives and many of the people they knew are woven into their fiction.

Saying that a novel is in some way a reflection of the life of the novelist is not new. Henry James, that anomaly and touchstone of American literature, said it in 1884 in "The Art of Fiction." He wrote, "A novel is in the broadest definition a personal, a direct impression of life." He then provides a metaphor which can help focus what I am attempting to say.

While discussing character and incident, James says, "it is an incident for a woman to stand up with her hand resting on a table and look out at you in a certain way." My attention is always drawn to that little "out." The woman does not merely "look at" you; she "looks out at."

Each of us "looks out at" the world in our own "certain way." Quite literally, a woman who is five feet tall sees the world differently from the way a woman of five feet seven sees it. We perceive the world differently, to give another example, if our eyes are myopic rather than normal.

Summary

That "looking out at" can be a metaphor for discussing the five authors here studied, the meaning of their work, and the meaning of all such work to American literature. The condition that Lebedeff, DeCapite, Mangione, Field, and Bell shared, the "certain way" in which they looked out at America, was marginality.

They, like all marginal persons, had to be concerned with three things: the culture of their ethnic group, the American culture they perceived, and their own identity. They were faced with finding --or making--their identity as a member of one or the other of those cultures, or neither.

The frequency with which these five marginal persons turned to the bildungsroman is indicative of their preoccupation with identity. The adolescent in search of his identity is a marginal person--on the margin between childhood and adulthood. The child of immigrant parents is in a matrix of marginality: between childhood and adulthood and between the culture his parents have brought with them and the culture he sees outside his ethnic group.

These five novelists were concerned with maturation, and they looked out at adulthood from the childhood experience they had, as everyone does, but they also looked out at American society from within an ethnic group. They could accept or reject that ethnic group; they could accept or reject what they saw of American society.

They could not reject their own early life or family experience, even though they might try. The angle of vision of early experience remained.

Their preoccupation with the story of adolescent growth indicates also that some of these authors had difficulty in finding their own identity and choosing their psychological home. Here, then, is the crux: how were they looking out at American society; i.e., from what angle of vision did they see America?

As the chapters on these five marginal writers have suggested, each of them made a choice to accept America. The differences in the choices were in the manner of their choosing based on the "certain way" each questioned what he or she saw. Lebedeff and Bell realized their marginality early, found their own identity, and then chose America with the full knowledge that the old ways were not thereby forgotten.

Lebedeff stood on the margin, seeing her ethnic group as marginal, and then seeing what choices were available to members of that group. Lebedeff's Anna chose America triumphantly, feeling free and feeling a part of the society in which she had found her place. But she brought with her symbols of her heritage: the Russian motifs she incorporated into the American clothes she designed.

DeCapite looked out at America as one of the poor, but he saw middle-class affluence as an American ideal. He worked his way into that society by the mobility device of education but found there shoddy values and shallow lives. He left the fate of several of his characters unresolved: Maria's Paul, Paul Barone and his friend Steve in _No Bright Banner_, and Stan Havranek in _The Bennett Place_.

DeCapite depicted the American mainstream as enervating,

destructive, or emasculating. He, like his characters, left it; unlike them, he did not flee from the arena of change and responsibility. He found his identity as a world citizen, transcending rather than solving his marginality.

Mangione and Field made the move to individual identity later in life, choosing America but still free to acknowledge their heritage. Mangione left his family in Mount Allegro, apparently to enter the larger society of America. But he alone, among the novelists studied, kept a focus on the old culture across the Atlantic, returning to it again and again, not committing himself to it, not able to let it go.

In the one early book in which identity is thematic, his hero, Stiano Argento, decides to be an autonomous person, but his story is told while he is in limbo on a ship at sea. When he is faced with the symbolic choice between his traditional, rather backward Sicilian wife and a liberal, activist mistress, he chooses to stay with his wife.

Of the five authors, Mangione was most concerned with the old home of his ethnic group; he wrote of the Sicilians in Rochester and those in Sicily, more than once, but he did not truly deal with America until after he symbolically murdered his Sicilianness in Night Search.

Then he could write of America as a place where some Italians live in America Is Also Italian and of an important part that he himself had in a unique event in American history, the Federal Writers Project. His work in progress An Ethnic at Large may be the work in which he will integrate his life, much as Field's Jacob's Son is an integration of his life.

Field looked at America, especially at the working poor, but he looked through the lenses of group identity, not solving his marginality. To look at America as revolutionary was to see himself as part of an activist group. Apparently, he took off the lenses of the sons of Jacob in his forties, but he could not choose an American identity for himself until he had shed all lenses and looked out at America as an autonomous person.

Thomas Bell disguised his Slovak origins by giving himself and some of his characters Anglo-Saxon names, but he never ceased to look out of his early childhood experiences of deprivation and exploitation. He never ceased asking why the powerful, mainstream Americans did not act out the ideals they professed. He never stopped speculating about the quality of life that could be lived if the affluence of America and the ideals of America were combined, when material comfort could assure constant psychological growth.

Early in his career, Bell spoke from that viewpoint of deprivation. He has Mike Strovenik say that America had taken away the lullabies of his people, their customs and values, and substituted paper pumpkins and hypocritical speeches. In that same novel, however, Bell worked out his identity as a writer. In his next book, he worked out his identity in a man-woman relationship. Finally, he displayed his identity as the child of immigrants by telling the story of his own people.

He looked out at America through the eyes of immigrants, Kracha and Mike Dobrejcak, and through the eyes of the children of immigrants, Mary Kracha and Dobie and Mikie. He saw the immigrants' aspirations; he saw the marginal persons' struggles. He also saw the American ideal and where it had not been achieved.

From then on, his heroes are not making their identities. They continue to grow and develop; they have hopes and plans, but they know who they are. They know, also, that they want to bring to reality the ideals of America, to bring to all Americans the necessary comforts that will allow them to discover what a man's life could be.

There are as many ways to look at America as there are persons who look. These five people have their marginality in common, but personal factors entered into each one's view. Lebedeff's was a sociological view: her analysis of group behavior provided her an answer. Mangione may have been hampered in finding his identity by his preoccupation with Sicily and helped by his career as a writer creating worlds in which to work out identity questions for his characters and himself.

Field's stance was ideological; he found his identity as a group member and only when he rejected all groups could he find himself and choose America.

Bell and DeCapite looked at American ideals from the point of view of the very poor. DeCapite saw the materialistic aspect, first as desirable and then as destructive. He also saw the idealism and went to work to return those ideals to American society by bringing them to the world.

Bell, too, saw material success as a possibility for everyone but as a means, not an end. His stance, it seems to me, was philosophical; he was the only one of the five who questioned the ultimates: the causes of human behavior, the reasons for human progress.

The bildungsroman that these five novelists wrote are different from other novels of adolescent growth, because the protagonists are never isolated, as was Holden Caulfield, for example. They belong to one or many groups: an extended family (their own or one they adopt), an ethnic group, a shop crew, the working class, and, finally, American society.

All through these novels, the adolescent interacts with his parents. He rejects them; he may even leave home. He must separate himself from them to make an identity; literally, to make a man of himself. He changes himself, and he changes his relationship with his parents.

When he finally returns, he relates to them as the adult he has become. He does not sneak into his home while his parents are asleep, nor relate only to his age peers; nor does he suffer isolation or break under the strain, as Holden did. On the contrary, he seeks his family and its values at holidays, at moments of stress, or when he is surfeited with the alien culture, as Paul Barone does in _No Bright Banner_.

Conclusion

The second part of this concluding chapter connects at this point. In a section called "The fiction of the forties and the existential crisis," Chester Eisinger writes:

> The theme of self-discovery that runs through the fiction of this period reveals the intense preoccupation of writers with the problem of the self; it reveals the struggle to define and shape a relationship between the self and American culture.[1]

This study and the first part of this conclusion have been

concerned with that relationship as evidenced in the lives and works of five authors. It remains to discuss their relationship to American literature and to consider if the place they have in it is different from the place they had 30 years ago. Is the message they have for the seventies different from the message they sent to their contemporaries?

The loosest definition of American literature is that it is literature written by any writer who is an American. Henry James, T.S. Eliot, and W.H. Auden make this an interesting definition to speculate about. Another definition is that American literature is a branch of English literature: it utilizes the same forms, participates in the same literary movements, and differs only--as some might insist--in the descriptions of landscapes and flowers.

A third theory, based on the Turnerian view of American history, is that American literature is the story of the lone hero, the self-made man, sometimes in and sometimes out of an American Eden. Leslie Fiedler offers a corollary in his theory that the pact with the Devil, the Faustian pact, has always been felt by American authors "as the essence of the American experience."[2]

After reading Bell, Field, and the others, a different definition can be posited: American literature details the truly American experience of deciding whether one is an American. To say that the experience of marginality is the quintessential American experience is putting the matter too strongly. To say that it is a pervasive experience is not.

Fiedler attributes a sense of marginality even to the most "American" of American writers. After introducing the idea of the

Faustian pact in relation to the work of Hawthorne and Melville, he proposes a margin on which American writers live:

> The American writer inhabits a country at once the dream of Europe and a fact of history; he lives on the last horizon of an endlessly retreating vision of innocence--on the "frontier," which is to say, the margin where the theory of original goodness and the fact of original sin come face to face.[3]

Whatever the metaphorical or mythical validity or value of this theory of marginality, there is enough actual marginality to cope with. Being an immigrant, or the child of immigrants, or a migrant within America has given a great many Americans the experience of looking out at America from within an ethnic group, a displaced group, or an exploited class.

In another sense, many Americans were made to feel displaced, if not marginal, by a restricted definition of American literature as literature of the East coast, the elite, the old-stock American. The definition of American literature as a branch of English literature also may have helped to foster a tendency to Anglo-conformism and a sense of displacement.

To teach the children of Slovak parents the Child ballads in elementary school and to ignore their own rich heritage of song is to diminish them and their heritage. To read Lincoln's words about slavery and not to read Frederick Douglass' is to know only one side of the American experience.

To label Conroy's <u>The Disinherited</u> and Bell's <u>Out of This Furnace</u> "proletarian literature" is to suggest that a story about the working class is a step-child of literature, not somehow equivalent to the story of an elite.

Thomas Bell suggested the unreality of the schooling the children of immigrants and workers were receiving when he wrote Mike Strovenik's diatribe against the phony holiday celebrations in the public schools and when he wrote Joel Panek's recollections of school learning as one thing and street knowledge as another. To make a definition of "American literature" that excludes certain novels, biographies, and songs is to displace not only the writers of those songs and stories but also the group or class or race from which those writers come.

Michael Novak witnesses to this displacement and its attendant guilt when he writes:

> If you are a descendent of southern and eastern Europeans, everyone else _has_ defined your existence. A pattern of "Americanization" is laid out. You are catechized, cajoled, and condescended to by guardians of good Anglo-Protestant attitudes. . . .
>
> The entire experience of becoming American is summarized in the experience of being made to feel guilty.[4]

The five ethnic novelists in this study, from their marginal position as the children of the so-called "New Immigrants," show American cities, farms, and mills, American families, ethnic groups, and classes in a way that only members of those groups and classes can. They are not uprooted Adams; they are here within a family, an ethnic group, a class. They did not come in time to see a virgin land or a machine in a garden. They saw a furnace that makes Americans as surely as it makes steel.

When their books were reviewed in the 40s, they were looked upon as stories, more or less interesting, more or less well written, more or less authentic. The reviewers generally did not perceive the identity search, the group orientation, the insight into the struggle to be a person in an America that ignored certain groups or exploited them or defined them as not quite American. These books can be read differently in this decade when autonomy is so valued and group membership so controversial.

As noted earlier, these five writers were chosen as subjects for this study after rather wide reading in novelists in the period who had marginal status. These five were chosen because they treated the themes of marginality and identity, and also because of the literary quality of their work.

Even among their work, however, the quality is not uniformly high nor is the subject matter uniformly relevant to our times. Lebedeff's one novel could perhaps be utilized in classrooms, because it so clearly presents the sociological view of marginality. Her characters flesh out the choices that can be made; they are not, however, stick figures nor is the novel lacking in artistry. Lebedeff's use of symbolism is quite good; her novel quite readable.

Field and Mangione are still writing and still concerned with the themes of ethnicity and identity. Jacob's Son is a summing up, as noted above, and is currently in print. It is the first novel of a trilogy, and I can only hope that it and the other two volumes will have a wide audience among those who want to include a very down-to-earth view of Jewish family life and the role it plays in the maturation of a young man who does not want to follow the paths tradition sets out for him.

Mangione, too, is contemplating a book about ethnicity; a summation of his life and thought. Mount Allegro was recently reprinted and stands as a rather sunny depiction of the Italian experience in America. It is aimed now for a juvenile audience and should do well as an antidote to the Mafia- and brutality-oriented works by others.

Maria, although not a great work, should be reprinted, also. It gives a less sunny picture than Mount Allegro but a picture of several neighborhoods and many individuals coping directly with the problems of acculturation and assimilation. DeCapite's Melting Pot view in Maria is simplistic and out of date, but the book has historical value because of his presentation of one theory of the process of Americanization.

The latter part of Out of This Furnace is likewise dated by its coloration of World War II patriotism, but it should be revived for its beautiful narration of the saga of three generations of Slovaks living in America. This novel would need no apologia for its inclusion in any canon of fine American writing. In addition, it would serve a consciousness-raising function for young people of Slovak ancestry and for other people who do not know the history of that group in America.

Out of This Furnace along with Field's "Cow" and some of his other farm stories could also serve to introduce young people to the labor movement: Field's work to point out the need for action and how grass roots actions were taken; Bell's work to give a more panoramic view of the progress of the labor movement from the unsuccessful Homestead strike to the beginnings of the CIO in the thirties.

The reprinting of Conroy's The Disinherited and the success of Stud Terkel's Hard Times indicate an interest in the Depression period. Bell and Field preserve not only that period but earlier times of depression, also.

American literature needs to include depictions of group life and group customs written by the members of each group: the songs of Mike Dobrejcak and the design motifs of Anna Borodin. It needs also the stories of groups in contact: the stories of extended families, of workers banding together, of immigrants arriving into a colony of their compatriots.

It needs narratives of those immigrants in contact with the Americans already here from the point of view of the immigrants and from the point of view of the old stock. An example of the latter is Willa Cather's My Antonia which portrays the vitality of Antonia Shimerda through the eyes of Jim, an old-stock American, who sees her vitality as an asset to America.

It is a paradox that the development of personal identity is most valued in the same moment that ethnicity is coming to greater acceptance throughout the world. An Anglo-French businessman took this emerging ethnicity as one theme in a New Year's Day essay on the question of the future of "One Europe."

> It will not be a culturally homogeneous Europe. I believe strongly in the Balkanization of cultures and think local cultures should be respected. The madness of the years since World War II, when everybody was trying to impose a sort of mid-Atlantic hamburger culture, is at an end. The French are becoming more French. The English are becoming more English.

> In America this is, of course, more than anywhere else. The Negroes are re-establishing their own culture, as are the Jews, Wasps, and everyone else.
>
> Worldwide, the need for people to identify with their own culture is being recognized for the first time. There is a European consciousness, but it doesn't replace the national one. . . . The Avignon Frenchman today feels European; he knows there is a general Old World culture, broken into subdivisions, which is different from that of America, the Far East or Russia. But he's mainly a Frenchman.[5]

The contradiction between the quest for identity and the interest in ethnicity is more apparent than real. Those two quests are parts of one trend toward acceptance of all aspects of one's self and one's heritage, for only by this acceptance can a person know his identity and function in strength and freedom.

When a society arranges its component groups into a hierarchical order, it diminishes members of those groups defined as "less" or "least." The price that is paid by blacks, for example, according to psychologist Price M. Cobb is "a lifelong draining of creative energy," and for whites, he has found, "a vague sense of some missing ingredient in their lives."[6]

Blacks are proclaiming that black is beautiful through essays, drama, music, novels, and poems, as well as in demonstrations. Chicanos are calling themselves *La Raza*, "the race." American Indians are calling themselves "Native Americans" and asking for the recognition that their many-faceted, rich, and ancient cultures deserve. Through these actions, all Americans are learning about these peoples, but more important, they are becoming aware that all peoples have beauty, a culture, a heritage.

Through this awareness, other groups will begin to define their own place in American society, history, and literature. Michael Novak's The Rise of the Unmeltable Ethnics is an effort to articulate the feelings of a Slovak Catholic scholar about being a Slovak and a Catholic in America, because, Novak writes, he has "regretted and keenly felt the absence of that sympathy for PIGS [Geno Baroni's unfortunate acronym for Poles, Italians, Greeks, and Slavs] which simple human feeling might have prodded intelligence to muster."[7]

Only if the group is not diminished can the members be whole. Only if the person is whole can he or she be autonomous and freely choose his group and his country. When thoughts and feelings are freed and the self redefined, Cobb writes, there is a reclaiming of "a natural love for others" and a release of energy which urges the person to change his life and which could "ultimately [change] the quality of American life."[8]

Novak expresses the same thought when he writes, "For it is in possessing our own particularity that we come to feel at home with ourselves and are best able to enter into communion with others."[9]

Lebedeff, DeCapite, and Bell worked out their identity before their middle years, Mangione and Field only later in life, but for each of them, with acceptance of personal identity came acceptance of America. They chose America, but they also accepted the other heritage that was theirs. It seems marginality can never be resolved; it can only be acknowledged.

The American climate is more and more one of acceptance; in a free America, ethnicity will not have to be resolved; all parts of a person's heritage will be acknowledged as part of that person's particularity. Such a "new pluralism" is already discerned by sociologists and historians of immigration.[10]

The theory of assimilation that Americans have talked about is the Melting Pot, but the one they have lived by is Anglo-conformism in a structurally pluralist society. To theorize that Germans, Irish, Serbians, Portuguese, and Anglo-Saxons could jump into a pot and emerge in a generation or two as a new man, an American, was far too simpleminded an explanation of a lengthy process.

As Glazer and Moynihan point out, the Melting Pot has worked to the extent that second and third and fourth generation Italian-Americans, Irish-Americans, Jewish-Americans, and African-Americans do not have the same attributes as their ancestors who came from Europe or Africa.

The theory of cultural pluralism or "immigrant gifts" was also simpleminded, especially when the great gift of language was eliminated as soon as possible and other gifts of clothing and cuisine were scorned.

Anglo-conformism, the Melting Pot, and cultural pluralism were theories based on a sociological view of human behavior, i.e., a view of persons acting in groups. Groups of people were to flow into the Melting Pot, for example, and a new kind of man, the American, was to pour out. A psychological orientation is pervasive today, however. Each person is trying to find his or her identity--ethnicity, sexual orientation, new, untried, non-stereotypical gender roles are all being considered.

Psychologists start from the premise that each person is OK and wants to feel OK. In a parallel trend, private people have taken up the notion that they are OK. If an outsider thinks members of a certain group are not OK, members of that group feel, on the contrary, that that their OKness enhances the group rather than being diminished by an outsider's opinion. The group receives its self-image from its members, not from a self-appointed outside group at the top of a self-defined hierarchical arrangement. This image is enhanced by pride in heritage, newly discovered or newly proclaimed.

A part of this same trend is the melting together of life styles and philosophies. The "immigrant gifts" are not merely displayed, they are imitated. Young whites are wearing dashikis and approximations of Afros. Young health food freaks of whatever color are experimenting with Chinese cooking.

The first theorizing about the Melting Pot was too simple; it is taking more generations to melt the immigrants than the people of the nineteenth and early twentieth centuries envisioned.

There is a progression in the theories of assimilation--from Anglo-conformism to the Melting Pot to cultural pluralism to structural pluralism to a theory of autonomous pluralism or "new pluralism," which says that each group has a culture, a heritage, a set of values, and in another sense, a value, which is OK, rich, worth preserving, and worth sharing.

Each person in that group is shaped by that heritage, those values; he or she is OK and has much to be proud of and much to share. Michael DeCapite apparently saw such an autonomous pluralism when he lived in Kashmir and learned about a rich and ancient way of life.

CONCLUSION

Literature could have a part in making this new, autonomous pluralism more actual to more Americans. A new definition of American literature could help form a new canon of American literature, one which will include the best songs and stories of all the peoples of America, their best gifts.

From that body of literature could come understanding, the acceptance of all heritages by people who see their own heritage represented there, and--in this era of personal growth--acknowledgement by everyone that all Americans are marginal persons who are constantly choosing their identity.

CHAPTER NOTES

Chapter I

[1]Rudolph J. Vecoli, "Ethnicity: a Neglected Dimension of American History," American Studies in Scandinavia, 4 (Summer 1970), 21.

[2]Ernece B. Kelly, ed., Searching for America, report of the NCTE Task Force on Racism and Bias in the Teaching of English (Urbana, Ill.: NCTE, 1972), xiii. See also Edward R. Weidlein, "Is English Healthy? Profession Isn't Sure," The Chronicle of Higher Education, 6 (January 10, 1972), 1,5; Maxine Dunfee, ed., Ethnic MOdification of the Curriculum. Report of a Conference, St. Louis, Missouri, 20-22 November 1969 (Washington: Association for Supervision and Curriculum Development, NEA, 1970).

[3]Kelly, p. xiii.

[4]Kelly, p. xiv.

[5]Myron Simon, "Ethnic Writers and Mainstream Literature," CEA [College English Association] Critic, 34, January 1972), 23. See also Charles A. Fenton, "The Lost Years of Twentieth Century American Literature," South Atlantic Quarterly, 59 (Summer 1960), 332-338.

[6]Howard Mumford Jones, "American Literature and the Melting Pot," Southwest Review, 26 (Spring 1941), 345.

[7]Chester Eisinger, Fiction of the Forties (Chicago: University of Chicago Press, Phoenix Book, 1965), p. 5.

[8]W. F. Thrall, Addison Hibbard, and C. H. Holman, A Handbook to Literature, 3rd ed., (Indianapolis: Odyssey Press paperback, 1972), pp. 408-409 passim.

[9]Thrall, pp. 388-389 passim.

[10]This method, independently arrived at, received reinforcement from R. W. B. Lewis, "Biography and Criticism: the Life and the Art," 13th Annual Joseph Warren Beach Memorial Lecture, University of Minnesota, April 29, 1971. See also John A. Meixner, "The Uses of Biography in Criticism," College English, 28 (November 1966), 108-113.

[11]Eisinger, p. 1. See also Robert E. Spiller, "Is Literary History Obsolete?" College English, 24 (February 1963), 345-351.

[12]Theodore C. Blegen, Grass Roots History (Minneapolis: University of Minnesota Press, 1947), p. 9.

[13]Theodore C. Blegen, Norwegian Migration to America, 1825-1860 (Northfield, Minn.: Norwegian-American Historical Association, 1931), p. v.

[14]Margaret Mead, Preface to Culture and Commitment: A Study of the Generation Gap (Garden City, N.Y.: Natural History Press paperback, 1970).

[15]Michael Novak, The Rise of the Unmeltable Ethnics (New York: The Macmillan Company, 1971), p. 140.

Chapter II

[1]Biographical information from the dust jacket flap of The Heart Returneth (Philadelphia: J. B. Lippincott Company, 1943); Garnet Warfel, "Knew It All the Time: Novelist Dreamed of Fame," Detroit News, 18 March 1943, n.p.; no author given, "Detroit Inspires Local Novelist as Epitome of Modern Life," Detroit Free Press, 28 March 1943, n.p.; Edwina LaMontagne, "Heads and Tragedy," Detroit News, 7 December 1965, n.p.; and letters from Vera Lebedeff dated 14 June, 20 September, 18 October 1972 and 19 June 1973.

[2]Lebedeff letter of 14 June 1972.

[3]"The Author," dust jacket of The Heart Returneth.

[4]Lebedeff letter of 20 September 1972.

[5]"Detroit Inspires Local Novelist as Epitome of Modern Life," Detroit Free Press, 28 March 1943, n.p.

[6]Lebedeff letter of 19 June 1973.

[7]Lebedeff letter of 14 June 1972.

[8]Lebedeff letter of 18 October 1972

[9]Vera Lebedeff, The Heart Returneth, p. 234.

[10]Lebedeff, The Heart Returneth, p. 262.

[11]Lebedeff letter of 19 June 1973.

Chapter III

[1]This biographical information and what follows are from Olga Peragallo, Italian-American Authors and Their Contribution to American Literature, (New York: S. F. Vanni, Publishers and Booksellers, 1949); Harry R. Warfel, American Novelists of Today, (New York: American Book Company, 1951); an obituary, "UN Aide Dies in Crash," New York Times, 22 January 1958, p. 8; and letters from Natalie Whiting DeCapite dated 19 and 20 April 1973.

[2]Michael DeCapite, "Louis Sullivan," Common Ground, 1 (Summer 1941), 73-80.

[3]1 (Autumn 1940), 29-36; 2 (Spring 1942), 50-52; (Winter 1942), 28-35.

[4]Anonymous [Michael DeCapite], "Labor on Foreign Fronts," New Republic, 106 (March 9, 1942) 331-332; "Europe Underground," (March 23, 1942), 397; "Labor on Foreign Fronts," (April 6, 1942), 461; "Europe Underground," (May 4, 1942), 605; and [signed] "Europe's Underground Press," The Nation, 154 (May 23, 1942), 592-595.

[5]Natalie Whiting DeCapite letter of April 20.

[6]N. W. DeCapite letter of April 19.

[7]Warfel, p. 114.

[8]N. W. DeCapite letter of April 19.

[9]Michael DeCapite, No Bright Banner (New York: The John Day Company, 1944), p. 87.

[10]M. DeCapite, No Bright Banner, p. 87.

[11]"UN Note to Correspondents No. 1715, 21 January 1958" and N. W. DeCapite letter of April 20.

[12]N. W. DeCapite letter of April 20.

[13]N. W. DeCapite letter of April 20.

[14]M. DeCapite, Maria (New York: The John Day Company, 1943). p. 85.

[15]M. DeCapite, Maria, p. 133.

[16]M. DeCapite, Maria, p. 232.

[17]M. DeCapite, Maria, p. 35.

[18]M. DeCapite, *Maria*. p. 106.

[19]M. DeCapite, *Maria*, p. 107.

[20]M. DeCapite, *Maria*, p. 108.

[21]M. DeCapite, *Maria*, p. 234.

[22]M. DeCapite, *Maria*, p. 304-305.

[23]M. DeCapite, *Maria*, p. 80.

[24]M. DeCapite, *Maria*, p. 135.

[25]M. DeCapite, *Maria*, p. 143.

[26]This is the episode that appeared in 1942 as "It Is Not So."

[27]M. DeCapite, *No Bright Banner*, p. 67.

[28]Professor Whitlock as encouraging mentor may be based on two women professors DeCapite had in college. One of them, who was very kind and encouraging, was apparently part of the source for Katherine Bennett in *The Bennett Place*, N. W. DeCapite letters of April 19 and 20.

[29]M. DeCapite, *No Bright Banner*, p. 270.

[30]M. DeCapite, *No Bright Banner*, p. 293.

[31]*Kirkus Service*, 12 (July 1, 1944), 285; Ruth Page, "Growth," New York *Times Book Review* (27 August 1944), p. 5; Herbert Kupferberg, New York *Herald Tribune Weekly Book Review* (27 August 1944), p. 6.

[32]Christine Walker, ed., "Reader Lives Within This Novel," Columbus *Dispatch*, 27 August 1944, p. 2F.

[33]Rose Basile Green, "The Italian-American Novel in the Mainstream of American Literature," address given at the Conference on the Italian-American Novel, Columbia University, October 25, 1969, p. 7.

[34]Green, p. 7.

[35]N.W. DeCapite mentions that Faulkner was a writer whom DeCapite "especially liked." Letter of 20 April.

[36]M. DeCapite, *The Bennett Place* (New York: The John Day Company, 1948), p. 141.

[37]M. DeCapite, Bennett Place, p. 205.

[38]M. DeCapite, Bennett Place, p. 94.

[39]N. W. DeCapite letter of 19 April.

[40]M. DeCapite, "Remarks for Award Luncheon 23 March," p. 1. The DeCapites were in India at the time of this luncheon, so Natalie DeCapite's father accepted the award for DeCapite. Letter of 20 April.

[41]M. DeCapite, Bennett Place, p. 137.

[42]A supercilious but perceptive comment by a British reviewer: "Despite irritating tricks and cliches of style--surely one can no longer talk of something being 'etched' against the sky?--he certainly can write." Simon Harcourt-Smith, "New Novels," New Statesman & Nation, 36 (August 21, 1948), p. 161.

[43]N. W. DeCapite letter of 20 April.

[44]M. DeCapite. "Remarks for Award Luncheon," p. 1.

[45]M. DeCapite, "Remarks for Award Luncheon," p. 1-2.

[46]M. DeCapite, "Application for Guggenheim," 1951, supplied with N. W. DeCapite letter of 20 April.

[47]N. W. DeCapite letter of 20 April.

[48]M. DeCapite, "the last section of unpublished novel - near the end. India," p. 446, supplied by N. W. DeCapite with letter of 20 April.

Chapter IV

[1]"Old Wine, New Bottle," Time, 41 (January 18, 1943), 104; Mary Ann Meyers, "Books and Authors," Delaware Valley Calendar (November 1965), p. 5.

[2]"Fontamara Revisited" was published under the pseudonym "Mario Michele."

[3]The story was given favorable mention by Jack Conroy in "An Anthology of WPA creative writing . . .", New Masses, 14 September 1937, Review and Comment column, p. 24, col. 2.

[4]Letter to the author from Jerre Mangione, March 12, 1973. Hereafter referred to as Mangione personal letter.

[5]Letter of Mangione to Gale Research, August 5, 1972, supplied to the author by Mangione.

[6]A copy of this statement was supplied to the author by Mangione with a letter dated August 25, 1972. Book titles appear in capitals as shown.

[7]Jerre Mangione, Mount Allegro (Boston: Houghton Mifflin, 1942, p. 1.

[8]Mangione, Mount Allegro, p. 232.

[9]Mangione, Mount Allegro, p. 235.

[10]Mangione, Mount Allegro, p. 245.

[11]Cf. Mangione, "Fascist Italy as I Saw It," Travel, 84 (November 1944), 5-9, 32.

[12]Maxine Block, ed., Current Biography: Who's News and Why (New York: H. W. Wilson Company, 1943), p.488

[13]Isaac Rosenfeld, "Allegro con Amore," The New Republic, 108 (March 22, 1943), 389. In Mangione's letter of 3/12/73 he notes that Rosenfeld's was "the most perceptive review [of Mount Allegro] . . . though he makes the mistake of assuming that Mount Allegro was written as a novel."

[14]Mangione, Reunion in Sicily (Boston: Houghton, Mifflin, 1950), p. 272.

[15]Mangione, Reunion in Sicily, p. 273.

[16]James M. Ethridge and Barbara Kopala, eds., Contemporary Authors (Detroit: Gale Research Company, 1966), Vol. 15-16, p.283; this biographical sketch notes that Mangione had more fables in progress. See "Oliver Arb," College Composition and Communication, 17 (1966) 59.

[17]Meyers, p. 5.

[18]Mangione, "Statement of Literary Purposes."

[19]Mangione, "The Writer's Secret Collaborator," in Psi Factors of Creativity, proceedings of a conference at St. Paul de Vence, France, June 16-18, 1969 (Parapsychology Foundation, 1970), pp. 51-63. Quotations are from a photocopy of the typescript--pages numbered 1-18--loaned to the author by Mangione.

[20]Mangione, America Is Also Italian (New York: G.P. Putnam's Sons, 1969), p. 89.

[21]Mangione, "Secret Collaborator," p. 8A

[22]Mangione, personal letter.

[23]Mangione, personal letter. Nina never appears in Night Search, but her personality is described. A similar character appears in Mangione's short story, "The Long Side of the Triangle," Esquire, 41 (April 1954), 48-49, 140-141.

[24]In an early short story "Tell Them She's Fine," Broun's Nutmeg (August 1, 1939), pp. 3-7, the narrator tells of being sent abroad--to Italy and Sicily--to write a series of articles. This narrator's name is Mike.

[25]Mangione, "Secret Collaborator," p. 10.

[26]Mangione, personal letter.

[27]Mangione, A Passion for Sicilians (New York: William Morrow and Company, Inc., 1968), p. 102. Ellipsis in the original.

[28]Peragallo, p. 145.

[29]Peragallo, p. 145.

[30]Mangione, America Is Also Italian, p. 97.

[31]Mangione, America Is Also Italian, p. 92-93.

[32]Mangione, "Secret Collaborator," p. 8A.

[33]Zena Hampson, "Jerre Mangione Remembers Rochester," Rochester Democrat and Chronicle, Upstate section, 4 March 1973, p. 16.

Chapter V

[1]Letter to the author from Ben Field, September 22, 1972, hereafter referred to as Field letter of September.

[2]Field letter of September.

[3]Field letter of September.

[4]Moses Bragin, in Joseph Auslander et al., eds., Copy 1930, (New York: D. Appleton and Company, 1930), p.340.

[5]Moe Bragin, "Cow," The Hound & Horn, 4 (July-September 1931), 559.

[6]Field letter of September.

[7]Headnote to Moe Bragin, "In Egypt," reprinted in Dorothy Scarborough, ed., Selected Short Stories of Today (New York: Farrar & Rinehart, Inc., 1935), p. 174.

[8]Field letter of September.

[9]Field letter of September.

[10]Field letter of September.

[11]Uncle Meyer is a composite figure: he was modeled after a Canadian uncle of Field's and a Canadian aunt with the admixture of some other elements. Field himself does not know the date of the original printing of "An Answer," per Field letter of September.

[12]Field letter of September.

[13]Ben Field, "Bialik Without Veils," Jewish Currents, 27 (May 1973), 16-19.

[14]Ben Field, The Cock's Funeral (New York: International Publishers, 1937), p. 27.

[15]Field letter of September. The character Cow was based on a friend of Field's, but not all the incidents in the story were based on real events. In regard to the red-haired wife of Cow, Field says, "There was a real red-haired girl, only in this sense: I have known red-haired women, and selected one as the model for the lean, attractive Mary Foley, Kathy O'Brien, and Cow's wife, although my friend married a brunette."

[16]Bragin, "Cow," p. 568.

[17]Bragin, "Cow," p. 568.

[18]Field, "An Answer for My Uncle," in Kerker Quinn and Charles Shattuck, eds., Accent Anthology; Selections from Accent, a quarterly of new literature 1940-1945 (New York: Harcourt, Brace and Company, 1946), p. 89.

[19]Field, The Outside Leaf (New York: Reynal & Hitchcock, 1943), p. 75.

[20]Field, Outside Leaf, p. 76.

[21]Field, Outside Leaf, pp. 227-228.

[22]Field, Outside Leaf, p. 100.

[23]Field, Outside Leaf, p. 225.

[24]Field letter of September.

[25]One of the vignettes in Moe Bragin's reportage, "In the Hudson Valley" is called "The Tompkins Place," but there is no apparent connection with the novel about Piper Tompkins. See B. A. Botkin, ed., Folk-Say IV, The Land Is Ours (Norman, Okla.: University of Oklahoma Press, 1932), pp. 181-188.

[26]Ben Field letter of March 10, 1973.

[27]Ben Field, The Last Freshet (Garden City, N.Y.: Doubleday 1948), p. 46.

[28]Field, Last Freshet, p. 173.

[29]Field, Last Freshet, pp. 268-270.

[30]Field, Last Freshet, p. 241.

[31]Field, Last Freshet, p. 237.

[32]Field, Last Freshet, p. 237. In answer to a query about Dr. Ormsby's rebellious, unconventional nature, Field replies, "Yes, Dr. Ormsby is a rebel in his way. He is modeled after the doctor friend who was a writer and an important member of the family circle, and also on a friend of mine, a classmate, who became a physician. Again a composite figure." Field letter of September.

[33]"In Egypt," a story of a family Passover gathering, appears again with different characters; a story about putting up light poles which appeared in the New Masses in 1935 is used again in Jacob's Son with Reuben, Michael, and Uncle Meyer as the pole-setters. Field letter of September. The reworking of "An Answer for My Uncle" was noted earlier.

[34]Field letter of September.

[35]Field letter of September.

[36]Peter Ellis, "Sights and Sounds," New Masses, 24 (November 2, 1937), 29. Field writes, "I do believe I used Green Fields as the name of Reuben Gross's farm because I had seen the play and liked it." Field letter of September.

[37]Novak, p. 247.

[38]The phrase "tree of life" appears in Gen. 3:22 and 24. Field notes, "The Tree of Life has been used frequently as the name of a Yeshivah, synagogue, or Talmud Torah. . . . The Torah to the orthodox Jew is the Tree of Life. The two rods around which the parchment of the Law, the Torah, is wound are called Trees of Life." Letter of September.

[39]Ben Field, Jacob's Son (New York: Crown Publishers, 1971), p. 333.

[40]Field, Jacob's Son, p. 332.

[41]Field letter of September.

[42]Field, Jacob's Son, p. 333.

[43]Field, Jacob's Son, p. 332.

[44]Field, Jacob's Son, p. 231.

[45]Field, Jacob's Son, p. 231.

[46]Field, Jacob's Son, p. 235.

[47]Field, Jacob's Son, p. 345.

[48]Field letter of September.

[49]Field letter of September.

[50]Field letter of September.

[51]Field letter of October 29, 1972.

[52]Field letter of October 29, 1972.

Chapter VI

[1]Philip Rahv, "Self-Definition in American Literature: Experience and Fulfillment," Commentary, 24 (December 1957), 534.

[2]Printed sources consist of a small blurb in Joseph Gaer, ed., Our Lives, American Labor Stories (New York: Boni & Gaer, Inc., 1948), p. 311, and an obituary, "Thomas Bell Dies; Novelist, was 56," New York Times, 18 January 1961, p. 33.

[3]Thomas Bell, In the Midst of Life (New York: Atheneum, 1961), p. 51.

[4]Bell, _In the Midst_, p. 73.

[5]Bell, _In the Midst_, p. 207.

[6]Bell, _In the Midst_, pp. 253-254 passim.

[7]Most of this information is in a letter to the author from Marie Benedetti Bell, widow of Thomas Bell, 28 January 1973. Hereafter referred to as M. B. Bell letter.

[8]Bell, _In the Midst_, p. 62.

[9]M. B. Bell letter.

[10]Bell, _In the Midst_, pp. 60-61.

[11]M. B. Bell letter.

[12]Anthony is living in Santa Cruz, California and collaborated with M. B. Bell in supplying information to the author, especially about Thomas' family and early life.

[13]M. B. Bell letter.

[14]M. B. Bell comments that it was "a very good film," letter of 28 January 1973. See review by Bosley Crowther, "'From This Day Forward,' RKO Film Starring Joan Fontaine, Has Premier at the Palace--Mark Stevens Is Featured," _New York Times_, 20 April 1946, p. 16.

[15]M. B. Bell letter.

[16]Thomas Bell, _In the Midst_, p. 206.

[17]Clippings of reviews supplied by the Library Museum of Performing Arts, New York Public Library at Lincoln Center, nearly all of them without page numbers; some with other data missing. All are dated 7 December 1943 unless otherwise noted. Kelcey Allen, "'The World's Full of Girls,'" _Women's Wear Daily_; Howard Barnes, "Below Par," _New York Herald Tribune_; Herrick Brown, "'The World's Full of Girls' Presented by Jed Harris at the Royale," _New York Sun_; John Chapman, "'The World's Full of Girls'--but It Still Could Use Some New Plays," _New York Daily News_; Robert Coleman, "'World [sic] Full of Girls' Is Disappointing," _New York Daily Mirror_, n.d.; Rowland Field, "Jed Harris Produces an Indecisive Drama," _Newark Evening News_, 8 December 1943; George Freedley, "'The World Is [sic] Full of Girls' Fails to Live Up to Expectations as Play," _New York Evening Telegraph_, 8 December 1943; Robert Garland, "Harris' New Offering Unveiled at Royale," _New York_

Journal American, p. 12; Ibee, "'World's Full of Girls,'" no name, n.d.; [Arthur] Kronenberger, "Almost But Not Quite," PM, 8 December 1943; Lewis Nichols, "The Play," New York Times, Amusement Section; Arthur Pollock, "Nunnally Johnson's 'The World's Full of Girls' Opens at Royale," Brooklyn Daily Eagle; Edgar Price, "Jed Harris Brings 'The World's Full of Girls' a Play by Nunnally Johnson, to the Royale Theatre--Comedy-Drama Based on Novel by Thomas Bell Is Disappointing," Brooklyn Citizen; Burton Rascoe, "What's Happened to the Nunnally Mind?" New York World-Telegram, p. 16; E.C.S., "'The World's Full of Girls,'" Christian Science Monitor; Wilella Waldorf, "Jed Harris' Latest: 'The World's Full of Girls,'" no name.

18M. B. Bell letter states "Jed Harris and Nunnally Johnson wrote and directed the script for laughs and it was a very bad script--he [Thomas Bell] did not approve of the way it was handled."

19Bell, In the Midst, pp. 112-113.

20Bell, In the Midst, p. 187.

21M. B. Bell letter.

22Bell, In the Midst, p. 87. Detachment and self-reliance as characteristics of creative persons were noted by Mary Henle, "The Birth and Death of Ideas," pp. 45-46, and Richard S. Crutchfield, "Conformity and Creative Thinking," p. 139 both in Howard E. Gruber et al., eds., Contemporary Approaches to Creative Thinking (New York: Atherton, 1962).

23Bell, In the Midst, pp. 223-224. It is interesting to note that Nicholas Berdayaev wrote in The Meaning of the Creative Act, "the way of creativeness is a way of sacrifice and suffering but it always means liberation from depression" (London: Victor Gollancz, Ltd., 1955), pp. 13-14.

24See Morris I. Stein, "Creativity and Culture," Journal of Psychology, 36 (1953), 311-322; A. H. Maslow, "The Creative Attitude," The Structurist, 3 (1963), 4-10 reprinted in R. L. Mooney and T. A. Razik, eds., Explorations in Creativity (New York: Harper and Row, 1967), pp. 43-54; and Maslow, Toward a Psychology of Being, 2nd ed. (Princeton: D. Van Nostrand Insight Book, 1968).

25Bell, In the Midst, p. 159.

26Bell, In the Midst, p. 160.

27Donald W. MacKinnon, "The Highly Effective Individual," Teachers College Record, 61 (April 1960), n.p. reprinted in Mooney and Razik, pp. 55-68.

[28]M. B. Bell letter.

[29]His wife's comment: "Thomas must have been born with the English language and his love of it." Letter.

[30]Thomas Bell, _The Second Prince_ (New York: G. P. Putnam's Sons, 1935), p. 284.

[31]Bell, _Second Prince_, p. 285.

[32]Bell, _Second Prince_, p. 127.

[33]Thomas Bell, _Out of This Furnace_ (Boston: Little, Brown and Company, 1941), p. 197.

[34]Bell, _In the Midst_, p. 51.

[35]Bell, _Second Prince_, p. 131.

[36]Bell, _In the Midst_, p. 155.

[37]Bell, _Second Prince_, p. 126.

[38]Bell, _Second Prince_, p. 127.

[39]Bell, _Second Prince_, p. 128.

[40]Bell, _Second Prince_, p. 129.

[41]Bell, _Second Prince_, pp. 128-129.

[42]Bell, _Second Prince_, p. 129.

[43]Bell, _Second Prince_, p. 130. The final passage quoted ends with the three dots in the original.

[44]Bell, _Second Prince_, pp. 132-133.

[45]Bell, _Second Prince_, p. 133.

[46]Bell, _Second Prince_, p. 207.

[47]Bell, _Second Prince_, p. 307.

[48]Bell, _Second Prince_, p. 308.

[49]Bell, _Second Prince_, pp. 304-305.

[50]Leslie A. Fiedler, Love and Death in the American Novel (Cleveland: World Publishing Company, Meridian Book, 1962), p. xix.

[51]Thomas Bell, All Brides Are Beautiful (Boston: Little, Brown and Company, 1936), p. 24.

[52]Fiedler, p. xix.

[53]Leo Gurko, The Angry Decade: American Literature and Thought from 1929 to Pearl Harbor (New York: Dodd, Mead and Company, 1947), p. 67.

[54]Gurko, p. 68.

[55]Gurko, p. 69.

[56]Gurko, p. 68.

[57]Bell, Out of This Furnace, p. 367. Michael Novak discusses a similar passage in Louis Adamic's work concerning his observation of "the destruction of the spirit of the immigrants," and recalls his own grandmother and "the dozens of black-draped women . . . who [were] like presences from some other, terrible world," in The Rise of the Unmeltable Ethnics (New York: Macmillan Company, 1971), pp. 75-78.

[58]Bell, Furnace, p. 196.

[59]Bell, Furnace, pp. 196-197 passim.

[60]Bell, Furnace, p. 196.

[61]Bell, Furnace, p. 198.

[62]Bell, Furnace, pp. 198-199.

[63]Bell, Furnace, p. 409.

[64]Bell, Furnace, p. 294.

[65]Bell, Furnace, p. 332.

[66]Bell, Furnace, p. 356.

[67]Bell, Furnace, p. 356.

[68]Bell, Furnace, p. 394.

[69]Bell, Furnace, pp. 410-411.

[70]Thomas Bell, Till I Come Back to You (Boston: Little, Brown and Company, 1943), pp. 213-214.

[71]Herrick Brown, n.p.

[72]Bell, In the Midst, p. 112.

[73]Thomas Bell, There Comes A Time (Boston: Little, Brown and Company, 1946), p. 29.

[74]Bell, There Comes A Time, p. 120.

[75]Bell, There Comes, p. 16.

[76]Novak, p. 55.

[77]Bell, There Comes, p. 17.

[78]Bell, There Comes, p. 16.

[79]Bell, There Comes, p. 170.

[80]Bell, There Comes, p. 265.

[81]Bell, There Comes, p. 267.

[82]Bell, There Comes, p. 267.

[83]Bell, There Comes, p. 268.

[84]Bell, There Comes, p. 272.

[85]Bell, There Comes, p. 179.

[86]Bell, There Comes, p. 138.

[87]Bell, There Comes, pp. 20-21 passim.

[88]Bell, "The Man Who Made Good in America," Mainstream, 1 No. 1 (Winter 1947) 15; reprinted in Gaer, Our Lives, American Labor Stories, pp. 16-23.

[89]Novak, p. 64.

[90]Novak, p. 139.

[91]Bell, In the Midst, pp. 91-92.

[92]Novak, p. 247.

[93]Bell, Second Prince, p. 297.

[94]Bell, In the Midst, p. 93.

Chapter VII

[1]"William Styron on Our Literature of Collision," interview by Philip Rahv, Modern Occasions, 1971 reprinted in Intellectual Digest, 2 (March 1972), 82-84.

[2]Ben Field letter of September 22, 1972.

[3]Ruth Page, "Growth," New York Times Book Review, 27 August 1944, p. 5.

[4]Robert M. Coates, "Terseness from the Left," New Masses, 23 (May 4, 1937), 31.

[5]John Norcross, "Spiritual Rebirth of a White Russian," Chicago Sun Book Week, 9 May 1943, p. 5.

[6]no author, no title, Detroit Free Press, 11 April 1943, n.p.

[7]Isaac Rosenfeld, "Allegro con Amore," New Republic, 108 (March 22, 1943), 388-389.

[8]Nathan L. Rothman, "Single Talent," Saturday Review of Literature, 29 (March 16, 1946), 16.

[9]Rosenfeld, p. 389.

[10]J. D. Ross, New York Herald Tribune Weekly Book Review, 16 May 1948, p. 4.

[11]Edmund Fuller, "Symbolic Ship of Outcasts," Saturday Review of Literature, 31 (May 29, 1948), 17.

[12]John Hyde Preston, "From the Still Center," New Republic, 109 (December 13, 1943), 862.

[13]Nina Brown Baker, "Tobacco Hero," New York Times Book Review (28 November 1943), p. 24.

[14]Baker, p. 24.

[15]Rothman, p. 16.

[16]Benjamin Appel, "Natural He-Man," Saturday Review of Literature, 31 (July 3, 1948), 15-16.

[17]Frances Woodward, "Above 149th Street," Saturday Review of Literature, 15 (November 7, 1936), 6.

[18]E. C. Beckwith, "Latest Works of Fiction," New York Times Book Review, 14 April 1935, p. 20.

[19]Clifton Fadiman, "Mixed Bag," New Yorker, 17 (April 5, 1941), 89.

[20]Margaret Wallace, "'Out of This Furnace' and Other Recent Works of Fiction," New York Times Book Review, 6 April 1941, p. 6.

[21]Henry Sydnor Harrison, "Adventures with the Editors: with a reexamination of an ancient inquiry: why are manuscripts rejected?" Atlantic Monthly, 113 (1914), 445-456.

[22]Bernard Berelson, "Who Reads What Books and Why?" Saturday Review of Literature, 34 (May 12, 1951), 7-8, 30-31.

[23]James Laughlin, ed., New Directions in Prose and Poetry 1941 (Norfolk, Conn.: New Directions, 1941), p. viii.

[24]Robert E. Cazden, "A Proposed Doctoral Program in Book-trade Research," Journal of Education for Librarianship, 7 (Spring 1967), 222-231.

[25]Allen Guttmann, The Jewish Writer in America: Assimilation and the Crisis of Identity (New York: Oxford University Press, 1971), p. 85.

[26]Mangione personal letter.

[27]M. B. Bell personal letter.

[28]N. W. DeCapite letter of 19 April.

[29]N. W. DeCapite letter of 19 April.

[30]Field letter of 22 September.

[31]Field letter of 22 September.

[32]Eisinger, p. 2.

Chapter VIII

[1]Eisinger, p. 308.

[2]Fiedler, p. xxii. Also see Thomas A. Krueger, "The Historians and the Edenic Myth: A Critique," The Canadian Review of American Studies, 4 (Spring 1973), 3-18.

[3]Fiedler, p. xxii.

[4]Novak, p. 62. Also see Rudolph J. Vecoli, "Born Italian: Color Me Red, White, and Green," Soundings (Spring, 1973), p. 122.

[5]James Goldsmith, contributor, "One Europe--Three Views," Newsweek, 1 January 1973, p. 24. Also see the Fall 1971 issue of The Antioch Review for Andrew Greeley, "The Rediscovery of Diversity," pp. 343-365; Jules Chametzky, "Regional Literature and Ethnic Realities," pp. 385-396; and "Observations" by the editor, Lawrence Grauman, Jr., pp. 295-298, 449; and the papers presented at a conference "The Global Dimensions of Ethnicity," under the auspices of the Minnesota Project on Ethnic America, Minneapolis, 17 May 1973. For a dissenting view, see Oscar Handlin, "The Half-Truth Way of Life," The New Leader, 1971, reprinted in Intellectual Digest, 2 (March 1972), 73-74.

[6]Cobbs, pp. 27, 28.

[7]Novak, p. 58.

[8]Cobbs, p. 28.

[9]Novak, p. xvi.

[10]Vecoli, "Born Italian," p. 123.

[11]Nathan Glazer and Daniel P. Moynihan, Beyond the Melting Pot (Cambridge, Mass.: MIT Press paperback, 1963), p. 13.

BIBLIOGRAPHY

N. A. "Some of the New Fiction," rev. of The Cock's Funeral, by Ben Field. New Republic, 91 (June 23, 1937), 202.

Allen, Kelcey. "'The World's Full of Girls,'" rev. of play. Women's Wear Daily, 7 December 1943.

Appel, Benjamin. "Natural He-Man," rev. of The Last Freshet, by Ben Field. Saturday Review of Literature, 31 (July 3, 1948), 15-16.

"The Author" dust jacket flap for The Heart Returneth. Philadelphia: J. B. Lippincott Company, 1943.

Baker, Nina Brown. "Tobacco Hero," rev. of The Outside Leaf, by Ben Field. New York Times, 28 November 1943, p. 24.

Barnes, Hazel E. "Philosophical Criticism," rev. article on Maurice Friedman To Deny Our Nothingness: Contemporary Images of Man. Contemporary Literature, 9 (Summer 1968), 427-30.

Barnes, Howard. "Below Par," rev. of The World's Full of Girls. New York Herald Tribune, 7 December 1943.

Barzini, Luigi. "Dangerous Acquaintances," rev. of A Passion for Sicilians, by Jerre Mangione. New York Review of Books, 13 (October 9, 1969), 46.

Beckwith, E. C. "Latest Works of Fiction," rev. of The Second Prince, by Thomas Bell. New York Times Book Review, 14 April 1935, pp. 19-20.

Bell, Marie Benedetti. Personal letter. January 28, 1973.

Bell, Thomas. All Brides Are Beautiful. Boston: Little, Brown & Company, 1936.

________. The Breed of Basil. New York: Robert M. McBride & Company, 1930.

________. "1800 Kisses a Year." McCall's, 77 (December 1949), 26-27, 127, 129-130.

________. "Fixing It Up for Joe." Colliers, 112 (December 18, 1943), 13, 66-68.

Bell, Thomas. "The Girl on the Porch." Colliers, 112 (November 27, 1943), 17, 64, 67-68.

_______. In the Midst of Life. New York: Atheneum, 1961.

_______. "Love Can Be a Habit." McCall's, 76 (March 1949), 24, 108-111.

_______. "The Man Who Made Good in America." Mainstream, a Literary Quarterly, Vol. 1, No. 1 (Winter 1947), 10-15. Reprinted in Joseph Gaer, ed., Our Lives, American Labor Stories. New York: Boni and Gaer, Inc., 1948, pp. 16-23.

_______. "One Year--Four Months." McCall's, 81 (October 1953), 42-43, 156-159, 163.

_______. Out of This Furnace. Boston: Little, Brown & Company, 1941.

_______. The Second Prince. New York: G. P. Putnam's Sons, 1935. Also known as Striker Godown. British edition, Eyre, 1936.

_______. "Some People Meet Too Soon." McCall's, 79 (September 1952), 48-49, 59-60, 70, 72, 78-79.

_______. "Tell Me That You Love Me." Ladies Home Journal, 63 (January 1946), 20-21, 137-138.

_______. There Comes a Time. Boston: Little, Brown & Company, 1946.

_______. Till I Come Back to You. Boston: Little, Brown & Company, 1943.

_______. "Young Man in a Hurry." Colliers, 113 (May 27, 1944), 27, 71, 73.

Berdayaev, Nicholas. The Meaning of the Creative Act. London: Victor Gollancz, Ltd., 1955.

Berelson, Bernard. "Who Reads What Books and Why?" Saturday Review of Literature, 34 (May 12, 1951), 7-8, 30-31.

Berger, Meyer. "The People of 'Little Italy,'" rev. of Mount Allegro, by Jerre Mangione. New York Times Book Review, 17 January 1943, p. 5.

Blegen, Theodore C. Grass Roots History. Minneapolis: University of Minnesota Press, 1947.

Blegen, Theodore C. Norwegian Migration to America, 1825-1860. Northfield, Minnesota: Norwegian-American Historical Association, 1931.

Block, Maxine, ed. Current Biography: Who's News and Why. New York: H. W. Wilson Company, 1943, pp. 488-490.

Bonosky, Phillip. "Ben Field's Sad and Beautiful Latest Novel," rev. of Jacob's Son, by Ben Field. Daily World, 8 September 1971, p. 8.

Bragin, Moe.[1] "Cake," The Midland, 17 (January-April 1931), 60-69.

________. "Cow." Hound & Horn, 4 (July-September 1931), 556-568. Reprinted in Granville Hicks, et al., eds. Proletarian Literature in the United States, An Anthology. New York: International Publishers, 1935, pp. 71-80 and in The Cock's Funeral.

________. "From an Eastern Farm," heading for two poems "Night" and "The Farmer's Daughter." Poetry, 37 (January 1931), 200-201.

________. "The Grasshopper Is Stirring." New Masses, 8, No. 3 (September 1932), 11-12. Reprinted under the name Ben Field in Proletarian Literature in the United States, An Anthology. New York: International Publishers, 1935, pp. 216-221.

________. "In Egypt." Opinion. Reprinted in Dorothy Scarborough, ed. Selected Short Stories of Today. New York: Farrar & Rinehart, Inc., 1935, pp. 174-188.

________. "In the Grass: A Story." New Masses, 7, No. 2 (June 1932) 21-23. Reprinted in The Cock's Funeral.

________. "In the Hudson Valley." In B. A. Botkin, ed., Folk-Say IV, The Land Is Ours. Norman, Oklahoma: University of Oklahoma Press, 1932, pp. 181-188.

________. "Journal of a Tour in America." The American Mercury, 26 (June 1932), 199-208.

________. "The Oppressed." New Masses, 7, No. 11 (May 1932), 20-21.

---

[1]Moses (or Moe) Bragin is the real name of Ben Field. Items printed under Bragin will be listed as such; those with Field by-line under Field.

Bragin, Moe. "Sentimental Cross-Country." In B. A. Botkin, ed., Folk-Say IV, The Land Is Ours. Norman, Oklahoma: University of Oklahoma Press, 1932, pp. 171-180.

________. "Thru the Sweaty Eye of a Needle." New Masses, 8, No. 3 (September 1932), 17-19.

________. "Work" (poem). Prairie Schooner, 4 (Summer 1930), 144-145.

Bragin, Moses. "A Japanese Kimono." Brith Sholom News. Reprinted in Joseph Auslander, et al., Copy 1930; Stories, Plays, Poems and Essays. New York: D. Appleton & Company, 1930, pp. 38-47.

Brandel, Marc. "DePereda, DeCapite," rev. of The Bennett Place, by Michael DeCapite. New York Times Book Review, 18 January 1948, p. 21.

"Briefly Noted: Fiction," rev. of Piper Tompkins, by Ben Field. New Yorker, 21 (February 9, 1946), 97.

________, rev. of Till I Come Back to You, by Thomas Bell. New Yorker, 19 (June 12, 1943), 78-79.

________, rev. of There Comes a Time, by Thomas Bell. New Yorker, 22 (July 20, 1946), 74.

________, rev. of The Bennett Place, by Michael DeCapite. New Yorker, 23 (January 17, 1948), 82.

________, rev. of The Ship and the Flame, by Jerre Mangione. New Yorker, 24 (June 12, 1948), 97.

Brookhouser, Frank. "Phila. [sic] Author in Sicily on Fellowship." The [Philadelphia] Evening Bulletin, 25 May 1965, p. 46B.

Brooks, John. "Sicily Recaptured," rev. of Reunion in Sicily, by Jerre Mangione. New York Times Book Review, 9 July 1950, p. 6.

Brown, Catherine Meredith. "Choked by Civilization," rev. of The Bennett Place, by Michael DeCapite. Saturday Review of Literature, 31 (January 17, 1948) 17.

Brown, Herrick. "'The World's Full of Girls' Presented by Jed Harris at the Royale," rev. of play. New York Sun, 7 December 1943.

Bruner, Jerome S. "The Conditions of Creativity." In Howard E. Gruber, et al., eds., Contemporary Approaches to Creative Thinking. New York: Atherton, 1962.

Burke, Kenneth. "Definition of Man." Hudson Review, 16 (Winter 1963-64), 491-514.

Cazden, Robert E. "A Proposed Doctoral Program in Booktrade Research." Journal of Education for Librarianship, 7 (Spring 1967), 222-231.

Chametzky, Jules. "Regional Literature and Ethnic Values." Antioch Review, 31 (Fall 1971), 385-396.

Chapman, John. "'The World's Full of Girls'--but It still Could Use Some New Plays," rev. of play. New York Daily News, 7 December 1943.

Coates, Robert M. "Terseness from the Left," rev. of The Cock's Funeral, by Ben Field. New Masses, 23 (May 4, 1937), 30-31.

Cobbs, Price M. "Ethnotherapy." Intellectual Digest, 11 (May 1972), 26-28.

Coleman, Robert. "'World [sic] Full of Girls' Is Disappointing," rev. of play. New York Daily Mirror, n.d. on clipping.

Conroy, Jack. "Even the Farm Animals Have Identities," rev. of Jacob's Son, by Ben Field. Kansas City Star, 1 August 1971, p. 4E.

________. "Review and Comment, An Anthology of WPA Creative Writing," rev. of American Stuff, An Anthology of Prose and Verse. New Masses, 14 September 1937, pp. 24-25.

Cooper, Arthur. "Writing for the Feds," rev. of The Dream and the Deal, by Jerre Mangione. Newsweek, 25 September 1972, p. 120.

Cordell, Richard. "Transplantation in America," rev. of Mount Allegro, by Jerre Mangione. Saturday Review of Literature, 26 (February 20, 1943), 10.

Crowther, Bosley. "'From This Day Forward,' RKO Film Starring Joan Fontaine, Has Premier at the Palace--Mark Stevens Is Featured," rev. of movie made from All Brides Are Beautiful, by Thomas Bell. New York Times, 20 April 1946, p. 16.

Crutchfield, Richard S. "Conformity and Creative Thinking." In Howard E. Gruber, et al., eds., Contemporary Approaches to Creative Thinking. New York: Atherton, 1962.

Davis, Robert Gorham. "The Continuing American Ideal: How Plural Is Our Culture?" Commentary, 25 (May 1958), 369-378.

DeCapite, Michael. "An American Story." '47 the Magazine of the Year, 1, No. 5 (July 1947), 48-49.

_______. "Application for Guggenheim." 1951. 2pp.

_______. The Bennett Place. New York: John Day Company, 1948.

_______. "The Bridge," [last chapter of Maria]. In John T. Frederick, ed., Out of the Midwest. New York: McGraw-Hill, Whittlesey House, 1944, pp. 89-99.

_______. "Decision." '47 The Magazine of the Year, 1, No. 4 (June 1947), 101-102.

_______. "Europe's Underground Press." The Nation, 154 (May 23, 1942), 592-595.

_______.[2] "Europe Underground." New Republic, 106 (March 23, 1942), 397.

_______.[2] "Europe Underground." New Republic, 106 (May 4, 1942), 605.

_______. "Honesty." Lamplighter (March 1938).

_______. "It Is Not So." Common Ground, 2 (Winter 1942), 28-35.

_______.[2] "Labor on Foreign Fronts." New Republic, 106 (March 9, 1942), 331-332.

_______.[2] "Labor on Foreign Fronts." New Republic, 106 (April 6, 1942), 461.

_______. "The last section of unpublished novel--near the end. India." p. 446.

_______. "Louis Sullivan." Common Ground, 1 (Summer 1941), 73-80.

_______. Maria, A Novel. New York: The John Day Company, 1943.

_______. No Bright Banner, A Novel. New York: The John Day Company, 1944.

[2]These were published anonymously.

DeCapite, Michael. "Remarks for Award Luncheon on 23 March" [1949]. 2pp.

_______. "The Story Is Yet To Be Told." Common Ground, 1 (Autumn 1940), 29-36.

_______. "War Comes to Little Italy." Common Ground, 2 (Spring 1942), 50-52.

DeCapite, Natalie Whiting. Personal letter. April 19, 1973.

_______. Personal letter. April 20, 1973.

Derleth, August. "Fine Regional Novel of Tobacco Leaf," rev. of The Outside Leaf, by Ben Field. Chicago Sun Book Week, 14 November 1943, p. 19.

"Detroit Inspires Local Novelist as Epitome of Modern Life," rev. of The Heart Returneth, by Vera Lebedeff. Detroit Free Press, 28 March 1943, n.p.

DeWolf, Rose. "Ethnic Heritage Should Not Pull Us Apart," commentary on Mangione and Mount Allegro. The Philadelphia Evening Bulletin, Focus section, 4 September 1972, p. 3B.

"The Director" [Mangione]. The Pennsylvania Gazette. Alumni magazine of University of Pennsylvania (December 1963), p. 7.

DuBois, William. "The Brooklyn Bridges," rev. of Till I Come Back to You, by Thomas Bell. New York Times Book Review, 20 June 1943, pp. 5, 10.

Dunfee, Maxine, ed. Ethnic Modification of the Curriculum. Report of a Conference on Ethnic Modification of the Curriculum, St. Louis, Missouri, 20-22 November 1969. Washington: Association for Supervision and Curriculum Development, NEA, 1970.

Edel, Leon. "Criticism and Psychoanalysis: Notes on the Two Disciplines." Chicago Review, 15, No. 2 (Autumn 1961), 100-109.

Eisinger, Chester E. Fiction of the Forties. Chicago: University of Chicago Press, Phoenix Book, 1965.

Eisinger, Chester E., ed. The 1940's: Profile of a Nation in Crisis. Garden City, New York: Anchor Books, 1969.

Ellis, Peter. "Sights and Sounds." New Masses, 24 (November 2, 1937), 29.

Erikson, Erik. "The Concept of Identity in Race Relations." Daedalus (Winter 1966). Reprinted in Ruth Miller and Paul J. Dolan, eds., Race Awareness: The Nightmare and the Vision. New York: Oxford University Press paperback, 1971.

Ethridge, James M. and Barbara Kopela, eds. Contemporary Authors. Detroit: Gale Research Company, 1966, Vols. 15-16, p. 283.

Faderman, Lillian and Barbara Bradshaw. Speaking for Ourselves, American Ethnic Writing. Atlanta: Scott, Foresman and Company paperback, 1969.

Fadiman, Clifton. "Mixed Bag," rev. of Out of This Furnace, by Thomas Bell. New Yorker, 17 (April 5, 1941), 89.

Farber, Marjorie. "In Search of an Author," rev. of Till I Come Back to You, by Thomas Bell. New Republic, 109 (July 26, 1943), 116.

Feld, Rose. "Russian Colony," rev. of The Heart Returneth, by Vera Lebedeff. New York Times Book Review, 11 April 1943, p. 7.

Fenton, Charles A. "The Lost Years of Twentieth Century American Literature." South Atlantic Quarterly, 59 (Summer 1960), 332-338.

Fiedler, Leslie A. Love and Death in the American Novel. Cleveland: World Publishing Company, Meridian Book, 1962.

Field, Ben. "An Answer for My Uncle." Accent. Also in Kerker Quinn and Charles Shattuck, eds., Accent Anthology; selections from Accent, a quarterly of new literature 1940-1945. New York: Harcourt, Brace & Company, 1946, pp. 87-98.

________. "Bialik without Veils." Jewish Currents, 27 (May 1973), 16-19.

________. The Cock's Funeral. New York: International Publishers, 1937.

"All Set"
"The Cock's Funeral"

Field, Ben. The Cock's Funeral (continued).
"Danbury Fair"
"The Hunt"
"Johnny Gets a Curve"
"Light"
"The Pitchfork Rises"
"Report"
"The Return"
"The Sheep Dip"
"We Will Remember"

________. "The Folk Image of Jacques Roumain," rev. of Masters of the Dew, by Jacques Roumain. Mainstream, A Literary Quarterly, 1, No. 3 (Summer 1947), 376-379.

________. Jacob's Son; a novel. New York: Crown Publishers, 1971.

________. The Last Freshet. Garden City, New York: Doubleday, 1948.

________. "A Lesson." The Cock's Funeral. Reprinted in Joseph Gaer, ed., Our Lives, American Labor Stories. New York: Boni & Gaer, Inc., 1948.

________. "The Market." In John Lehmann, ed., New Writing. London: Lawrence & Wishart, 1937; New York: Alfred A. Knopf, 1937, pp. 225-234.

________. "Maxie Genof." In Max Lieber, ed., The American Century. Reprinted in a German translation, Leipzig: VEB Leipziger Druckhaus [Leipzig Publishers, Inc.], 1957.

________. "The New Housekeeper." The Cock's Funeral. Reprinted in Nicholas Moore, ed., The PL Book of Modern American Short Stories. Ipswich: Editions Poetry; London, Nicholson & Watson, 1945, pp. 149-160.

________. The Outside Leaf. New York: Reynal & Hitchcock, 1943.

________. Personal letter. September 22, 1972.

________. Personal letter. October 29, 1972.

________. Personal letter. March 10, 1973.

________. Piper Tompkins. Garden City, New York: Doubleday & Company, Inc., 1946.

Field, Ben. "Virge Doggity," [first chapter of The Last Freshet]. Mainstream, a Literary Quarterly, 1, No. 4 (Fall 1947), 462-467.

________. "Whom the Ox Gored." In James Laughlin, ed., New Directions in Prose and Poetry 1941. Norfolk, Conn.: New Directions, 1941.

Field, Rowland. "Jed Harris Produces an Indecisive Drama." Newark Evening News, 8 December 1943, rev. of play.

Fisher, Vardis. "The Novelist and His Background." Western Folklore, 12 (January 1953), 1-8.

Forman, Henry James. "Once the Playground of the Gods," rev. of Reunion in Sicily, by Jerre Mangione. The Saturday Review, 33 (July 1, 1950), 8-9.

Freedley, George. "'The World Is [sic] Full of Girls' Fails to Live Up to Expectations as Play," rev. of play. New York Evening Telegraph, 8 December 1943.

Freedman, Morris and Carolyn Banks. American Mix: The Minority Experience in America. Philadelphia: J. B. Lippincott Company, 1972.

Fuller, Edmund. "Symbolic Ship of Outcasts," rev. of The Ship and the Flame, by Jerre Mangione. Saturday Review of Literature, 31 (May 29, 1948), 17.

R. G. [biography of Jerre Mangione] Saturday Review of Literature, 33 (July 1, 1950), 8.

Gaer, Joseph, ed. Our Lives, American Labor Stories. New York: Boni & Gaer, Inc., 1948.

Garland, Robert. "Harris' New Offering Unveiled at Royale," rev. of play. New York Journal American, 7 December 1943, p. 12.

Glazer, Nathan. "The Immigrant Groups and American Culture." Yale Review, 48 (March 1959), 382-397.

Glazer, Nathan and Daniel Patrick Moynihan. Beyond the Melting Pot. Cambridge: MIT Press paperback, 1963.

Goldsmith, James. "One Europe--Three Views." Newsweek, 1 January 1973, pp. 23-25.

Goodale, Ralph Hinsdale. "Six Kinds of Frustration," rev. of The Bennett Place, by Michael DeCapite. Christian Century, 65 (May 12, 1948), 448.

Grauman, Lawrence, Jr. "Observations" [editorial]. The Antioch Review, 3 (Fall 1971), 295-98, 449.

Greeley, Andrew M. "The Rediscovery of Diversity." The Antioch Review, 3 (Fall 1971), 343-365.

Green, Rose Basile. "The Italian-American Novel in the Mainstream of American Literature." Address given at the Conference on the Italian-American novel at Columbia University, October 25, 1969. Printed in John M. Cammett, ed., The Italian-American Novel, Proceedings of the Second Annual Conference of the American Italian Historical Association, Columbia University, October 25, 1969, pp. 1-5.

Gross, Theodore L., ed. A Nation of Nations, Ethnic Literature in America. New York: The Free Press paperback, 1971.

Gurko, Leo. The Angry Decade: American Literature and Thought from 1929 to Pearl Harbor. New York: Dodd, Mead & Company, 1947.

Guttmann, Allen. The Jewish Writer in America: Assimilation and the Crisis of Identity. New York: Oxford University Press, 1971.

Guzzardi, Walter, Jr. "South and West of Palermo," rev. of A Passion for Sicilians, by Jerre Mangione. Saturday Review, 51 (November 9, 1968), 39.

Hampson, Zena. "Jerre Mangione Remembers Rochester." Rochester Democrat and Chronicle, Upstate section, 4 March 1973, pp. 4-5, 7-12, 14, 16.

Handlin, Oscar. "The Half-Truth Way of Life." The New Leader, 1971. Reprinted in The Intellectual Digest, 2 (March 1972), 73-74.

Harcourt-Smith, Simon. "New Novels," rev. of The Bennett Place, by Michael DeCapite. New Statesman & Nation, 36 (August 21, 1948), 161-162.

Harrison, Henry Sydnor. "Adventures with the Editors: with a re-examination of an ancient inquiry: why are manuscripts rejected?" Atlantic Monthly, 113 (1914), 445-456.

Haslam, Gerald W. Forgotten Pages of American Literature. Boston: Houghton Mifflin Company, 1970.

Hatch, Robert. "Danilo Dolci's Vita," rev. of A Passion for Sicilians, by Jerre Mangione. Nation, 207 (December 2, 1968), 602.

Hauser, Marrianne. "Italian-Americans," rev. of Maria, by Michael DeCapite. New York Times Book Review, 10 January 1943, p. 5.

Henle, Mary. "The Birth and Death of Ideas." In Howard E. Gruber, et al., eds., Contemporary Approaches to Creative Thinking. New York: Atherton, 1962.

Hicks, Granville, et al., eds. Proletarian Literature in the United States, An Anthology. New York: International Publishers, 1935.

Hindus, Maurice. "Steel in the Melting Pot," rev. of Out of This Furnace, by Thomas Bell. Saturday Review of Literature, 23 (May 3, 1941), 11.

Hoffman, Frederick J. "Dogmatic Innocence: Self-Assertion in Modern American Literature." Texas Quarterly (University of Texas), 6, No. 2 (Summer 1963), 152-162.

Hogan, William. "The Turbulent Writers Project," rev. of The Dream and the Deal, by Jerre Mangione. San Francisco Chronicle, 25 August 1972, n.p.

Hume, Robert D. "Intention and the Intrinsic in Literature." College English, 29 (February 1968), 355-365.

E. C. I. "Artistry," rev. of The Bennett Place, by Michael DeCapite. Christian Science Monitor, Magazine Section, 7 February 1948, p. 12.

Ibee. "'World's Full of Girls,'" rev. of play. Name of paper and date not on clipping.

Inglis, Ruth A. "An Objective Approach to the Relationship between Fiction and Society." American Sociological Review, 3 (August 1938), 526-531.

Jackson, Joseph Henry. "A Woman Who Failed," rev. of The Bennett Place, by Michael DeCapite. San Francisco Chronicle, 27 February 1948, p. 18.

Jelliffe, R. A. "Unflinching Record of One Who Met Death Boldly," rev. of In the Midst of Life, by Thomas Bell. Chicago Sunday Tribune, Magazine of Books, 3 September 1961, p. 2.

Jones, Howard Mumford. "American Literature and the Melting Pot." Southwest Review, 26 (Spring 1941), 329-346.

Kaplan, Harold. "Dismantling America." American Journal, 1, No. 3 (February 13, 1973), 18-23.

Kazin, Alfred. "Love without Money," rev. of All Brides Are Beautiful, by Thomas Bell. New York Times Book Review, 1 November 1936, p. 7.

________. "'Mr. Pirate' and Other Recent Works of Fiction," rev. of The Cock's Funeral, by Ben Field. New York Times Book Review, 11 July 1937, p. 7.

Kelly, Ernece B., ed. Searching for America: A Publication of the Conference on College Composition and Communication and the National Council of Teachers of English, NCTE Task Force on Racism and Bias in the Teaching of English. Urbana, Ill.: NCTE, 1972.

Kneller, George. The Art and Science of Creativity. New York: Holt, Rinehart & Winston, 1965.

Kronenberger, [Arthur]. "Almost But Not Quite," rev. of play. PM, 8 December 1943.

Krueger, Thomas A. "The Historians and the Edemic Myth: A Critique." The Canadian Review of American Studies, 4 (Spring 1973), 3-18.

Kupferberg, Herbert. Rev. of No Bright Banner, by Michael DeCapite. New York Herald Tribune Weekly Book Review, 27 August 1944, p. 6.

________. Rev. of The Outside Leaf, by Ben Field. New York Herald Tribune Weekly Book Review, 28 November 1943, p. 23.

LaMontagne, Edwina. "Heads and Tragedy." The Detroit News, 7 December 1965.

Laughlin, James, ed. New Directions in Prose and Poetry 1941. Norfolk, Conn.: New Directions, 1941.

Lebedeff, Vera. The Heart Returneth. Philadelphia: J. B. Lippincott Company, 1943.

_______. Personal letter. June 14, 1972.

_______. Personal letter. September 20, 1972.

_______. Personal letter. October 18, 1972.

_______. Personal letter. June 19, 1973.

Lee, Charles. "The Bitter Dilemma of the DP," rev. of The Ship and the Flame, by Jerre Mangione. New York Times Book Review, 16 May 1948, p. 5.

Lewis, R. W. B. "Biography and Criticism: The Life and the Art." Thirteenth annual Joseph Warren Beach Memorial lecture, University of Minnesota, April 29, 1971.

MacBride, James. "Bank Clerk Hits Back," rev. of There Comes A Time, by Thomas Bell. New York Times Book Review, 21 July 1946, p. 4.

MacKinnon, Donald W. "The Highly Effective Individual." Teachers College Record, 61 (April 1960), n.p. In Ross L. Mooney and Taher A. Razik, eds., Explorations in Creativity. New York: Harper & Row, Publishers, 1967, pp. 55-68.

Mackler, Bernard and Franklin C. Shontz. "Creativity: Theoretical and Methodological Considerations." Psychological Record, 15 (1965), 217-238.

Mangione, Jerre. "America Bella," [excerpts from Mount Allegro]. In B. A. Botkin, eds., Sidewalks of America, Folklore, Legends, Sagas, Traditions, Customs, Songs, Stories and Sayings of City Folk. Indianapolis: Bobbs-Merrill, 1954, pp. 56-58.

_______. America Is Also Italian. New York: G. P. Putnam's Sons, 1969.

_______. Bibliography (partial) sent to Anne Commire of Gale Research, August 5, 1972.

_______. "Cry, David, Cry." Four Winds Literary Quarterly, 1954.

_______. The Dream and the Deal: The Federal Writers' Project 1935-1943. Boston: Little, Brown, 1972.

Mangione, Jerre. "The Enticements of Erice." Sicilia, 47 (1965), 57-63.

________. "An Excess of Personality," rev. of From Caesar to the Mafia, by Luigi Barzini. Philadelphia Sunday Bulletin, 4 July 1971.

________. "Fascist Italy as I Saw It." Travel, 84 (November 1944), 5-9, 32.

________ [Mario Michele, pseud.]. "Fontamara Revisited." New Republic, 91 (May 26, 1937), 69-71.

________. Foreword to David S. Stern, Seventy [book of verse]. Philadelphia, 1960.

________. "Getting Acquainted with My Sicilian Relatives." Travel, 71 (October 1938), 10-13, 46.

________. "Growing Up Sicilian," rev. of What the Ancients Said, by Lou D'Angelo. Book Week, 4 April 1971.

________. "Half-Bitter, Half-Sweet," rev. of Half-Bitter, Half-Sweet, An Excursion into Italian-American History, by Alexander DeConde. New York Times Book Review, 6 February 1972, p. 41.

________. "He Believed in the Qualities of the Common Man," rev. of A Traveler in Two Worlds, by Maurice Hindus. New York Times Book Review, 26 September 1971, p. 55.

________. "Interview with Philip Roth." Pennsylvania Review, 1 (1966), 29-39.

________. "Italian-Americans Spice the Melting Pot." Philadelphia Sunday Bulletin, 11 May 1970.

________. "Let's Resurrect 'Federal One.'" The Chronicle of Higher Education, 7 (May 21, 1973), 12.

________. Letter to Anne Commire of Gale Research, August 5, 1972.

________. Life Sentences for Everybody. New York: Abelard-Schuman, Ltd., 1965.

________. "The Long Side of the Triangle." Esquire, 41 (April 1954), 48-49, 140-141.

Mangione, Jerre. "Man with the Cracked Derby." In American Stuff; An Anthology of Prose and Verse by Members of the Federal Writer's Project. New York: Viking Press, Inc., 1937, pp. 153-157.

________. "A Man's Best Audience Is His Horse." Globe: Intimate Journal, [Milwaukee, Wisconsin] May 1938, pp. 30-33, 114.

________. Mount Allegro. Boston: Houghton Mifflin, 1942.

________. Night Search. New York: Crown Publishers, 1965.

________. "Oliver Arb." College Composition and Communication, 17 (1966), 59.

________. "Palermo." Harper's Bazaar, October 1937.

________. A Passion for Sicilians: The World Around Danilo Dolci. New York: William Morrow and Company, Inc., 1968.

________. Personal letter. March 12, 1973.

________. "Le Professeur et La Vie Intellectuelle." Information and Documents, November 15 - December 1, 1953, pp. 48-53.

________. Reunion in Sicily. Boston: Houghton Mifflin Company, 1950.

________. The Ship and the Flame. New York: A. A. Wyn Publisher, Current Books, Inc., 1948.

________. "Statement of Literary Purposes."

________. "Stephen Crane's Unpublished Letters." The Chap Book (Syracuse University Literary Magazine), 1930.

________. "Tell Them She's Fine." Broun's Nutmeg (New Canaan, Conn.) 1 August 1939, pp. 3, 7.

________. "Troubled Time in Marriage," rev. of No Resting Place, by Eugene Mirabelli. The [Philadelphia] Sunday Bulletin, Book Section (Sec. 5), 30 July 1972, p. 7.

________. "The Vestal." Era, 1 (1964), 32-39.

________. "Water Girl." Broun's Nutmeg (New Canaan, Conn.) 1 July 1939, p. 5.

Mangione, Jerre. "Why Can't Johnny Write?" The [Philadelphia] Sunday Bulletin Magazine, 15 September 1963, pp. 8-9.

________. "The Writer's Secret Collaborator." In Psi Factors of Creativity, proceedings of an international conference held at St. Paul de Vence, France, June 16-18, 1969. Parapsychology Foundation, 1970, pp. 51-63. Quotations are from a Xerox copy of the typescript--pages numbered 1-18--on loan from Mangione.

Sister Mary Marguerite. Rev. of Jacob's Son, by Ben Field. Best Sellers, 31 (July 15, 1971), 178.

Maslow, Abraham H. "The Creative Attitude." The Structurist, 3 (1963), 4-10. Reprinted in Ross L. Mooney and Taher A. Razik, eds., Explorations in Creativity. New York: Harper & Row, Publishers, 1967, pp. 43-54.

________. Toward a Psychology of Being (2nd edition). Princeton: D. Van Nostrand Company, Insight Book, 1968.

Match, Richard. "Drama of the Small-Town Schizoid," rev. of The Last Freshet, by Ben Field. New York Times Book Review, 11 April 1948, p. 22.

Mead, Margaret. Culture and Commitment: A Study of the Generation Gap. Garden City, New York: Natural History Press paperback, 1970.

Meixner, John A. "The Uses of Biography in Criticism." College English, 28 (November 1966), 108-113.

Meyers, Mary Ann. "Books and Authors," [about Mangione]. Delaware Valley Calendar [of Camden, N.J.] November 1965, p. 5.

Newell, Allen, J. C. Shaw and Herbert A. Simon. "The Processes of Creative Thinking." In Howard E. Gruber, et al., eds., Contemporary Approaches to Creative Thinking. New York: Atherton Press, 1962.

"New Novels," rev. of Till I Come Back to You, by Thomas Bell. Time, 41 (June 14, 1943), 104.

Nichols, Lewis. "The Play," rev. of play. New York Times, Amusements section, 7 December 1943.

Norcross, John. "Spiritual Rebirth of a White Russian," rev. of The Heart Returneth, by Vera Lebedeff. Chicago Sun Book Week, 9 May 1943, p. 5.

"Note to Correspondents," [about DeCapite]. Note No. 1715, 21 January 1958. United Nations Headquarters.

Novak, Estelle Gershgoren. "'New Masses' Five Yearly Indexes of the Poetry, Fiction, Criticism, Drama and Reviews for the Years 1929 through 1933." Bulletin of Bibliography, 28 (July-September 1971), 89-108.

Novak, Michael. The Rise of the Unmeltable Ethnics: Politics and Culture in the Seventies. New York: The Macmillan Company, 1971.

"Old Wines, New Bottle," rev. of Mount Allegro, by Jerre Mangione. Time, 41 (January 18, 1943), 103-104.

Page, Ruth. "Growth," rev. of No Bright Banner, by Michael DeCapite. New York Times Book Review, 27 August 1944, p. 5.

Passantino, Myrtle. Rev. of A Passion for Sicilians, by Jerre Mangione. America, 120 (January 11, 1969), 48.

Peragallo, Olga. Italian-American Authors and Their Contribution to American Literature. New York: S. F. Vanni, Publishers and Booksellers, 1949.

Pollock, Arthur. "Nunnally Johnson's 'The World's Full of Girls' Opens at Royale," rev. of play. Brooklyn Daily Eagle, 7 December 1943, n.p.

Preston, John Hyde. "From the Still Center," rev. of The Outside Leaf, by Ben Field. New Republic, 109 (December 13, 1943), 860, 862.

Price, Edgar. "Jed Harris Brings 'The World's Full of Girls' a Play by Nunnally Johnson, to the Royale Theatre--Comedy-Drama Based on Novel by Thomas Bell Is Disappointing." Brooklyn Citizen, 7 December 1943.

Rahv, Philip. "Self-Definition in American Literature: Experience and Fulfillment." Commentary, 24 (December 1957), 530-537.

Rascoe, Burton. "What's Happened to the Nunnally Mind?" rev. of play. New York World-Telegram, 7 December 1943, p. 16.

Redman, Ben Ray. "The Man in the Street and Life," rev. of Till I Come Back to You, by Thomas Bell. Saturday Review of Literature, 26 (June 26, 1943), 7.

Review of The Heart Returneth, by Vera Lebedeff. Detroit Free Press, 11 April 1943, n.p.

Review of No Bright Banner, by Michael DeCapite. Kirkus Service, 12 (July 1, 1944), 285.

Rosenfeld, Isaac. "Allegro con Amore," rev. of Mount Allegro, by Jerre Mangione. New Republic, 108 (March 22, 1943), 388-389.

Rosengarten, Frank. "Alienation, the Quest for Identity, and Social Conflict in the Italian-American Novel." In John N. Cammett, ed., The Italian-American Novel, Proceedings of the Second Annual Conference of the American-Italian Historical Association, Columbia University, October 25, 1969, pp. 11-17.

Ross, J. D. Rev. of The Ship and the Flame, by Jerre Mangione. New York Herald Tribune Weekly Book Review, 16 May 1948, p. 4.

Rothman, Nathan L. "The Return to the Soil," rev. of The Outside Leaf, by Ben Field. Saturday Review of Literature, 26 (December 11, 1943), 13.

________. "Single Talent," rev. of Piper Tompkins, by Ben Field. Saturday Review of Literature, 29 (March 16, 1946), 16.

E. C. S. "'The World's Full of Girls,'" rev. of play. Christian Science Monitor, 7 December 1943.

Samachson, Dorothy. "When Uncle Sam Put Culture on the Payroll," rev. of The Dream and the Deal, by Jerre Mangione. Chicago Daily News, Panorama section, 27-28 January 1973, p. 11.

Schrag, Peter. "The Decline of the WASP." Harper's, 240 (April 1970), 85-91.

Simon, Myron. "Ethnic Writers and Mainstream Literature." CEA Critic, 34 (January 1972), 20-25.

Simon, Myron, ed. Ethnic Writers in America. New York: Harcourt Brace Jovanovich, Inc., 1972.

Spiller, Robert E. "Is Literary History Obsolete?" College English, 24 (February 1963), 345-351.

Steadman, R. W. "A Critique of Proletarian Literature." North American Review, 247 (Spring 1939), 142-152.

Stein, Morris I. "Creativity and Culture." Journal of Psychology, 36 (1953), 311-322.

Sylvester, Harry. Rev. of The Cock's Funeral, by Ben Field. New York Herald Tribune Books, 25 April 1937, p. 10.

Tebbel, John. A History of Book Publishing in the United States; Vol. I: The Creation of an Industry, 1603-1865. New York: R. R. Bowker, 1972.

"Thomas Bell Dies; Novelist, Was 56." New York Times, 18 January 1961, p. 33.

Thrall, W. F., Addison Hibbard, C. H. Holman. A Handbook to Literature (3rd edition). Indianapolis: Odyssey Press paperback, 1972.

Trilling, Diana. "Fiction in Review," rev. of Maria, by Michael DeCapite and Mount Allegro, by Jerre Mangione. Nation, 156 (January 23, 1943), 137.

________. "Fiction in Review," rev. of The Outside Leaf, by Ben Field, Nation, 158 (January 8, 1944), 51-52.

Troy, William. "Shorter Notices," rev. of All Brides Are Beautiful, by Thomas Bell. Nation, 143 (November 28, 1936), 640.

Tumin, M. "Obstacles to Creativity." ETC, 11 (Summer 1954), 261-271.

"UN Aide Dies in Crash" [about DeCapite]. New York Times, 22 January 1958, p. 8.

Vecoli, Rudolph J. "Born Italian: Color Me Red, White, and Green." Soundings (Spring 1973), pp. 117-123.

________. "Ethnicity: a Neglected Dimension of American History." American Studies in Scandinavia, 4 (Summer 1970), 5-23.

________. "The Italian-American Literary Subculture: an historical and sociological analysis." In John N. Cammett, ed., The Italian-American Novel, Proceedings of the Second Annual Conference of the American Italian Historical Association, Columbia University, October 25, 1969, pp. 6-10.

K. W. "The New Books; Fiction," rev. of The Second Prince, by Thomas Bell. Saturday Review of Literature, 12 (August 24, 1935), 21.

Waldorf, Wilella. "Jed Harris' Latest: 'The World's Full of Girls,'" rev. of play, name of paper not on clipping, 7 December 1943.

Walker, Christine, ed. "Reader Lives within This Novel," rev. of _No Bright Banner_, by Michael DeCapite. _Columbus Dispatch_, 27 August 1944, p. 2F.

Wallace, Margaret. "'Out of This Furnace' and Other Recent Works of Fiction," rev. of _Out of This Furnace_, by Thomas Bell. _New York Times Book Review_, 6 April 1941, pp. 6-7.

Warfel, Garnet. "Knew It All the Time: Novelist Dreamed of Fame," rev. of _The Heart Returneth_, by Vera Lebedeff. _Detroit News_, 18 March 1943.

Warfel, Harry R. _American Novelists of Today_. New York: American Book Company, 1951.

Weeks, Edward. "The Peripatetic Reviewer," rev. of _The Heart Returneth_, by Vera Lebedeff. "The Atlantic Bookshelf," _Atlantic_, 172 (July 1943), 129.

Weidlein, Edward R. "Is English Healthy? Profession Isn't Sure." _The Chronicle of Higher Education_, 6 (January 10, 1972), 1, 5.

Weisberg, Paul S., and Kayla J. Springer. "Environmental Factors in Creative Function." _Archives of General Psychiatry_, 5 (December 1961), 64-74. In Ross L. Mooney and Taher A. Razik, eds., _Explorations in Creativity_. New York: Harper & Row, 1967, pp. 120-134.

Wheelock, John Hall, ed. _Editor to Author: The Letters of Maxwell E. Perkins_. New York: Charles Scribner's Sons, The Scribner Library, 1950.

"William Styron on Our Literature of Collision" interview by Philip Rahv. _Modern Occasions_, 1971. Reprinted in _Intellectual Digest_, 2 (March 1972), 82-84.

"Wins Award of Friends of American Writers." _Publishers Weekly_, 155 (March 26, 1949), 1445.

Woodburn, John. "Homeward Bound," rev. of _The Ship and the Flame_, by Jerre Mangione. _New Republic_, 119 (October 4, 1948), 25.

Woodward, Frances. "Above 149th Street," rev. of _All Brides Are Beautiful_, by Thomas Bell. _Saturday Review of Literature_, 15 (November 7, 1936), 6.

ADDENDUM TO BIBLIOGRAPHY

Bell, Thomas. Out of This Furnace with an Afterword by David. P. Demarest, Jr. Pittsburgh: University of Pittsburgh Press, 1976.

______. Out of This Furnace. New York: Liberty Book Club, Inc., 1950.

______. "Six Months to Live," [2 chapters from In the Midst of Life]. Reader's Digest, 71 (July 1961), 94-98.

Berko, John F. "Thomas Bell (1903-1961) Slovak American Novelist," Cleveland, Rome: Slovak Institute, 1975; offprint from Slovak Studies, XV. [lists some bibliographical items not in the bibliography in this volume].

Blicksilver, Edith. The Ethnic American Woman: Problems, Protests, Lifestyle. Dubuque, Iowa: Kendall-Hunt Publishing Co., 1978.

Burch, Betty Ann. "East European Writers in America: Four Cases." in Charles A. Ward et al, eds., Studies in Ethnicity: The East European Experience in America. Boulder: East European Monographs, No. LXXIII, 1980, pp. 233-254. [Richard Bankowsky, Thomas Bell, Ben Field, Vera Lebedeff].

Butcher, Philip. The Ethnic Image in Modern American Literature: 1900-1950. Washington, D.C.: Howard University Press, 1984, 2 volumes.

______. The Minority Presence in American Literature, 1600-1900. Washington, D.C.: Howard University Press, 1977, 2 volumes.

Demarest, David P., Jr. From These Hills, From These Valleys; Selected Fiction about Western Pennsylvania. Pittsburgh: University of Pittsburgh Press, 1976. [contains a chapter from Out of This Furnace and notes on Thomas Bell].

Field, Ben. "A Dissent on 'Herzog,'" Jewish Currents, 19, April 1965, 19-21.

Harap, Louis. Creative Awakening: The Jewish Presence in Twentieth Century American Literature, 1900-1940. Contributions in Ethnic Studies No. 17. Westport, CT: Greenwood Press, 1987.

______. The Image of the Jew in American Literature: From Early Republic to Mass Immigration. Philadelphia: the Jewish Publication Society of America, 1974.

______. In the Mainstream: The Jewish Presence in Twentieth Century American Literature, 1950s-1980s. Westport, CT: Greenwood Press, 1987. [Ben Field is included in a list on page 10.].

Jason, Sonya. "Good Times and Love; the Life of Thomas and Marie Bell." _Slovakia_, XXV, (1975), 18-27.

Mangione, Jerre. _An Ethnic at Large: A Memoir of America in the Thirties and Forties_. New York: G.P. Putnam's Sons, 1978. First paperback edition Philadelphia: University of Pennsylvania Press, 1983.

_______. _Mussolini's March on Rome_. New York: Franklin Watts, Inc., 1975.

"Mangione, Jerre Gerlando" [entry] _Supplement to Who's Who in America_. 45th edition, 1989-1990, p. 756.

Rubenstein, Annette T. "Ben Field Begins a Trilogy," _Jewish Currents_, 25, November 1971, 29-32.

Schappes, Morris U., "American Jewish Life and Literature," _Science and Society_, 53, Fall 1989, 341-346. [Review of Louis Harap, _Creative Awakening_ and _In the Mainstream_, noting short shrift given to Ben Field.]

[Schappes, Morris U.]. "In Memoriam: Ben Field (1901-1986)," _Jewish Currents_, 40 (October 1986), 27.